Disney's

1 | WONDERFUL WORLD OF KNOWLEDGE

DISNEY'S

Wonderful World of Knowledge

THE DANBURY PRESS

THE DANBURY PRESS

a division of Grolier Enterprises, Inc.

ROBERT B. CLARKE	*Publisher*
ROBERT G. BARTNER	*Marketing Director*
GILBERT EVANS	*Creative Director*
JACK JAGET	*Design*
THE STONEHOUSE PRESS	*Production Supervision*

ARNOLDO MONDADORI EDITORE

MARIO GENTILINI	*Editor-in-Chief*
ELISA PENNA	*Supervising Editor*
GIOVAN BATTISTA CARPI CLAUDIO MAZZOLI	*Illustrators*
SERGIO FRUGIS	*Author*

"Disney's WONDERFUL WORLD OF KNOWLEDGE"
is an updated and enlarged English version of
an encyclopedia heretofore printed in the Italian language by
ARNOLDO MONDADORI EDITORE, MILAN
and entitled (in English Translation) "Disney ENCYCLOPEDIA"

CONTENTS

LIFE UNDER THE JUNGLE TREES

Hello, boys and girls. I'm your friend Donald Duck. Isn't it wonderful that I am going to travel with you all over the world! I feel really honored because the editors of this first volume of our encyclopedia have chosen me to be your guide. It's hard to believe but it's true. We are going together to meet some animals. The animals we are going to meet are called mammals. Mammals are animals that nurse their young on milk. I mean, of course, that all mammal mothers do that. And another thing to remember, boys and girls, is this: all, or nearly all mammals, have fur; almost all have four legs. By the way, mammals are the animals that we know best. Dogs and cats, horses and cows, rabbits and squirrels are all mammals. So are the fierce lions and tigers, the huge elephants, and the towering giraffes. You may be surprised to learn that the bat, which flies around at night, is also numbered among the mammals. And so are we. Human beings are mammals, too.

I really can't tell you why the authors have chosen me, though. Unless . . . oh, now I remember. It all began, no doubt, when I was on my way home by way of Africa and found a lost, hungry, and yowling leopard cub in my arms. It was quite an occasion, because I mistook the cub for a plain, ordinary cat. I took it home to meet Tabby. What a mistake! Tabby behaved very badly indeed and

ran to the doghouse for protection. So, of course, I had to take the cub back where I found him. Or he found me. In my opinion, I was chosen to be your guide because of my experience with the lost cub. Anyway, that's enough of an introduction. Let's get going. After you, dear friends, naturally.

Just look! We can see a huge green ocean stretching before us: the jungle. For thousands of miles, there are millions of plants all twisted and tangled around one another, overhead and underfoot. Here are plants that grow so fast and so high that they block out everything in their way as they reach for the light of the sun. But some plants are able to exist even in the shade of bigger plants.

Jungles are different, according to the continents on which they are found. Let's start with a visit (just a quick one) to that large band of permanent jungle surrounding the earth. It lies between the tropics and extends from South America to Central Africa. It touches part of India and the Far East and reaches Northern Australia. My comments about this green jungle belt will be brief. I mention it in order to help you to understand better the animals who live there.

A jungle is a region, usually hot, with very thick vegetation—oh, you've no idea how thick it is. Twisted branches form a roof that is sometimes 100 feet thick! The animals that live there have a very

developed ability to climb, jump, and grip. They climb and jump from branch to branch. They go up and down the trunks of trees with all the skill and ease of monkeys. And that is odd, for that is exactly what most of them are—monkeys!

These animals that can climb so well are the primates. The word "primate" comes from a Latin word meaning "first." Carolus Linnaeus, the Swedish naturalist, made up the name. The primates are the highest order of animals and include monkeys, apes, and man. But you must remember that of all the primates, the mon-

This spider monkey is among the strangest of the animals of the Amazon jungle of South America. He got his name because if he were spread out flat he would look like a spider. This lively monkey has very long arms and legs and an even longer tail. He can grasp with his tail or wrap it around a tree trunk. Spider monkeys are able to cross a river by forming a living chain. They hold each other by the tail and swing from a treetop on one side of the water to a treetop on the other side. The funny little face on the opposite page belongs to the squirrel monkey.

10

keys are best suited to the life of a climber. If we look at their paws, we see that their hands have five fingers. Their feet have toes, which really look more like fingers. These fingerlike toes are a help in grasping objects, as are their tails. The tail, wrapped around the limb of a tree, is an aid in climbing and in swinging from one branch to another. The monkeys of South Africa and Asia do not have grasping tails, but some other kinds of animals do. The opossum, the kinkajou, some rats and other rodents, the scaly anteater, and the bearcat of Indochina are among those animals that use their tails for grasping. I could tell you a tale about tails, but I won't.

THE HOWLER MONKEYS

Boys and girls, there is something important I want to talk about before we continue. I just wish you had a chance to

hear the thousands and thousands of sounds in the jungle. At first glance, you might think that there was not very much animal life in the tropical forests because nothing would be moving. This is so because the animals hide, especially during the day. They hide themselves among the leaves, behind tree trunks, in treetops, and even in the thick underbrush. Nor

Opposite, top: This beautiful yellow-chested creature is found throughout Africa, in wooded areas near rivers and streams.

Opposite, bottom: The chimpanzee is very intelligent. He is the only animal capable of using tools, though they may be very simple ones. He uses sticks to pry out termites and worms. He picks leaves from which to drink.

Left: When he is up in a tree, the orangutan is very strong and acts like Tarzan. It is another matter when he is on the ground because his legs are short and weak. His name in the Malaysian language means "man of the forest." The orangutan is most often found on the islands of Borneo and Sumatra. Below: This monkey has sideburns and a white beard.

would you hear very much. A great deal has been written about the silence of the jungle during the daytime. For a long while nothing is heard. Suddenly a shrill scream of a bird breaks the silence. Then there is the chatter of a squirrel, the droning flight of an insect, the crash of a giant tree as it falls to the earth below, or the quiet sound of a nearby river. Otherwise silence. But it is at night that the animal world comes to life. Then, as if by magic or the wave of an invisible baton, the deafening music of a jungle concert begins. The locusts with their metallic noises, the croaking of the tree frogs, the shrill screaming of thousands of parrots getting ready to sleep, and the loud cries of the howler monkeys—all join the chorus.

These howler monkeys are found mainly in South America. That is, they are found in the trees of the jungles of South America. They rarely leave their treetops, even for a drink. The howler monkey quenches his thirst by licking damp leaves. It's easy to understand why he is called a howler monkey. His cry is as loud as the great roar of an angry lion, and can be heard almost a half-mile away. Can you imagine a troop of 30 or 40 howler monkeys in full voice? These monkeys live together in groups and can defend themselves by howling when danger threatens. The noise that they make is absolutely terrifying. It is enough to wake the dead.

But in spite of all this, when I see a baby howler monker, my heart melts. When they are just born, the little ones hug their dear mother's breast. During the first year of their life, they ride on her back, just the way a tiny monkey does. After this year, the little monkey takes his first steps along the branches of the giant trees. Now he becomes very brave. Because he knows that if he falls, the whole troop—all of his aunts, uncles, and cousins—will rush to his aid, all howling as loudly as they can.

At nightfall it is as though the jungle were bewitched. The jaguars and the fierce leopards begin to roar. Later on, in

the dead of night, only a chorus of tree frogs and insects remind us that the jungle is really alive. And then towards dawn, there is a new round of sounds. It is that of the early risers going in search of food and drink. After that, once more in the fullness of the day, the jungle is quiet.

That's right, boys and girls. During the day we could walk in the jungle for hours without seeing even the shadow of any of the animals we are looking for. If we take a more careful look, however, we may see the fresh print of a paw on the ground. The most visible tracks in the African jungle are those left by the warthogs and other wild pigs that follow elephant trails and feed on roots and fallen leaves. You'll also find the tracks of the baboon who follows the warthog, to eat his leftovers, and to get the worms and scorpions unearthed in the tracks. Picture yourself in the very heart of a jungle or tropical rain forest. Above your head is a never-ending green roof made of twisted branches and leaves of trees—so thick that almost no light comes through. The air will seem very still to you, and it is, because the wind, like the light, barely penetrates. This is why the depths of a rain forest are almost always completely still. If you ever get a chance to walk through a jungle, you'll soon see what I mean.

Because there is very little breeze to carry scents, many animals of the jungle seldom use their sense of smell. Several animals also have little use for their sense of sight because of the dim light in the jungle. So they are quite unlike the animals who live in the open spaces. For example, the okapi that lives in the jungles of Central Africa is not nearly as keen-sighted as his cousin, the antelope, that roams the prairies of the same region.

However, I want to point out to you that the hearing of the okapi is highly developed. And there's also nothing wrong with the hearing of the tree monkeys. When they want to communicate with each other they simply open their mouths and yell.

But let's move on. It is easy to see that the thick growth in the jungle makes it hard for animals to move swiftly on the ground. For this reason, the larger mammals are at some disadvantage when it comes to defending themselves or attacking other animals. But we must remember the great strength of these larger mammals. Just think of the elephant, the buffalo, and the leopard. Why, the leopard can knock down his victim with just one sweep of his heavy and powerful paw. And as for the elephant, there's almost no limit to his power!

15

Here are the eyes of a tiger, a puma, and an African lynx—although the lynx seems to have his eyes closed! They are three beautiful and fierce animals. At 1½ months of age the tiger cub learns his first hunting lore. At about 2 years, he leaves his "parents" home to lead his own independent life in the jungles of Asia. The puma purrs as he breathes in and out and sounds like a contented house cat, of whom he is a distant relative. He hunts at night and is the terror of small animals. A caracal, or African lynx, is the most elegant of the lynx family.

THE JUNGLE CATS

Now we are going to come face to face with some of the most beautiful animals in the world. But don't let yourself be bewitched by their eyes: they can be soft, angry, piercing, of a shining and brilliant color somewhere between blue, green, and yellow. These wonderful eyes belong to the tiger, the leopard, the jaguar, and the puma—the fierce lords of the dense jungle.

Magnificent in a yellow-gold coat striped with black, the tiger makes his way with grace through the Asian jungle. The tiger walks lightly in spite of his nearly 550 pounds. He moves easily over the ground, careful to step on stones, craftily placing his back paws in the tracks made by his front paws in order to confuse any possible follower. The tiger is above all a suspicious animal. He is so suspicious and cunning that no one, not even the cleverest and most fearless of hunters can take him by surprise—not even when the tiger sleeps. A night creature, the tiger begins hunting at sundown. And it is then that his large, shining eyes scan the forest land so that he will be ready to glide like a snake or leap like an acrobat onto practically any animal that comes within reach. There is but one ani-

mal of the forest, the elephant, which can be careless about the tiger, and cross his path without fear. But no other living creature of the jungle is able to escape the bloodthirsty killer tiger.

The tiger is a good swimmer. In fact, his daily diet, which consists of between 65 and 100 pounds of "meat," includes water creatures as well. The tiger eats standing up, always ready for an unpleasant surprise. In this he differs from the cheetah or the lion, who recline while eating, their muzzles buried deep in their —plates! Oops, I mean prey.

Tiger cubs, trained by their mother, soon learn to find their own food and to avoid pitfalls and traps. This is why, as soon as they are out on their own, they go their way in the jungle with an air of challenging the whole world.

According to a Malayan belief, the surest way to be caught by a tiger is to speak his name. For this reason, in Malaysia and surrounding regions, the tiger is not called a tiger, but "the one with the whiskers." So, remember boys and girls, if you should ever come across a tiger, don't say his name. I'm just fooling.

Opposite page: Here are two jaguars who look very different at first glance. The male is black, which is rare for a jaguar, and the female is gold with black spots. Actually, the male is not really jet black. In a certain light, you can see spots under his dark coat. Some people believe that eating a jaguar will give them courage.

Above: The lynx is nimble, patient, and swift. He is supposed to have the best eyesight of any animal. The lynx differs from the other jungle cats in having a short tail and ears with tufts on the tips. The lynx lives on almost every continent. The Canada lynx and the bobcat live in North America.

19

Another fierce animal of the cat family, this one found on the American continent, is the puma. Like the tiger, the puma is an animal that strikes with his paws.

Well, boys and girls, why the puzzled look? I'm sure you've heard of the puma and the cougar, too. The puma, the cougar, the American mountain lion, and the bear cat, even the silver cat, are all different names for the same magnificent animal. The puma is a roving bandit that is fleet and tireless, and very powerful. He is also, ahem! something of a coward when he is chased or feels cornered by man or dogs. In captivity, that is, in zoos, the puma becomes quite tame, so much so that he permits visitors to approach. Remember, boys and girls, the next time you're at your favorite zoo, be sure to look up your friend the puma and say hello. He's really not such a bad fellow, especially when there are some heavy iron bars between you and him.

Hey, watch out! Those two animals coming toward us are jaguars—a rare black jaguar and his beautiful spotted lady. The jaguar is the real lord of the Amazon jungle. He is a powerful swimmer and prefers the jungle river banks where he finds most of his prey. He likes to stretch out on a branch overhanging the water, waiting for some large fish to swim by. He fishes for his meal with his paw. He also goes after the capibara, which is a large water rodent found in the rivers of South America. Some of the teeth of the capibara are used as ornaments by the people who live near the rivers. The jaguar will also hunt tapirs, anteaters and alligators, if he cannot find anything he really prefers. His other victims are usually domestic animals. He often jumps boldly into cattle enclosures under the very eyes of the watchman guarding the herds.

The male jaguar, though often fierce with other animals, is a good father. He is ready to feed and protect his children at all times. The female jaguar usually gives birth to a litter of one to three cubs and looks after them lovingly for about 2 years. After that, the cubs are left on their own.

Let's end this parade of beautiful animals with the leopard found mostly in Africa and Asia. He is such a splendid, fierce, and fearless animal. The leopard, with great patience, is able to lie in wait for hours and hours and hours. Balanced on a tree branch, once he has caught the scent of a possible victim, he will pounce on it like a hawk on his prey.

So, let's leave the crouching leopard

At the left is a baby macaca, the kind of monkey most used in scientific experiments. The monkeys who live on the Rock of Gibraltar belong to this family. There are about 30 of them in Gibraltar and they are the only wild monkeys in Europe.

and really push on. There is someone making a lot of awful noise down there in the jungle. It isn't really a bellow—no, it is more like trumpeting. So we'll say goodbye to the lovely, huge, green and golden eyes of the jungle cats and be on our way.

THE BIGGEST OF THE LAND ANIMALS

That was a close shave! We just missed being bumped into by an elephant, and I personally almost lost my feathers, my spare ones included! Did you see what a race of giants they are, these elephants? One just doesn't joke with such a heavyweight. To think that at birth, poor babies, they weigh about 200 pounds. But don't worry, after a few years those little ones will have no trouble at all carrying their 6 tons or so through the jungle as though it were nothing at all. And they won't break an arm or leg doing it, either.

An elephant's foot has five toes, and the elephant walks, if you can call it that, on the tops of these, or rather on the

nails. The bones of his feet are protected by a sort of spongy sole, which rests on the ground. This sole is so elastic and springy that when the elephant rests all of his 6-ton weight on it, it gives like a sponge, expanding when the foot is lifted. It's like a shock absorber!

Another feature of the elephant that is interesting is his trunk. He can sense which way the wind is blowing by lifting his trunk up in the air like a periscope.

At birth, an elephant is pink in color and is about 3 feet in height. In a few short hours he is able to stand, and in a few days can walk—with mamma's help. The mother is both kind and brave, and at the first sign of danger, she grabs her baby by the trunk and carries him to safety.
The elephants shown here are African. See the large ears, so different in size from the ears of elephants found in India. As you can see, Dumbo comes from Africa!

And he also uses it to pluck fruit, branches, and leaves when it time to eat. He uses it not only for eating but for drinking, too. He can draw sand up into his trunk and spray the sand over his back as a kind of daily anti-insect treatment. Each day the elephant eats about 500 pounds of fruit, leaves, and barks of all kinds. It is good to know that the elephant is a vegetarian—this big fellow is not likely to go after the likes of you and me, my friends.

If you look at an elephant's ears, you will be able to tell whether he comes from India or Africa! An African elephant has enormous, floppy ears. The Asian elephant's ears are much smaller—in fact the Asian elephant is smaller altogether than his African relative.

The Asian elephant is good-natured and is a hard worker. We said worker, and we meant it, for he is often called the "tractor" of the jungle. He is able to pull up to 5 tons of lumber without much effort. He works all day long with his mahout. The mahout is the man who rides on the elephant's head, guides him, and tells him what to do and when. He is a good fellow, our busy Asian elephant.

Oops, I almost forgot the pygmy elephant. He is small—rarely taller than 5 feet and lives in the tropical jungles of

Africa. He differs from other elephants in that he is hairy—nearly as hairy as a monkey. All in all, should you ever come across him, you'll see how cute a fellow he is.

We might have known it. The elephants had hardly passed out of sight before the warthog appeared in their tracks, hoping to pick up a meal without any effort. What can you do? The elephants allow Mr. Warthog to do it, and they go on to other things. From the

height of their wisdom the elephants know that in life it is good to be kind with those less fortunate. Finding his meals ready-made is small consolation for the warthog, who, as one can guess from his name, is hardly a raving beauty. This wild hog is about 3 feet at the shoulder and does in fact have warts on his snout. What's more, when he senses danger he flees as fast as he can, his tail in the air like a flag. A hunter who is following almost has to stop and laugh because the hog looks so ridiculous.

In the jungles of South America, we come next to the giant armadillo of Brazil.

He is really a big fellow, measuring 5 feet in length and weighing in at around 140 pounds. There also is his cousin the "pampas" armadillo, or "three-banded" armadillo, as well as the "nine-banded" Mexican armadillo, or the "cautious one," because he digs many different homes in order to confuse his enemies. All three of these armored boxes have one thing in common: a hard, banded hide that snaps shut. This well-sealed armor is the animal's best protection. In this way he can escape any enemy except the people of the region, who have found a way of roasting the armadillo, armor and all.

We must also meet the giant anteater, surely one of the strangest animals there is on earth. He belongs to the same group as the armadillo, but instead of armor, he is covered by thick fur. The giant anteater has a long, almost cylindrical snout, with a very small mouth. His tongue is

The elephants pictured on the opposite page live in India. They need more than 300 quarts of water a day—100 for drinking and 200 to pour over themselves.

Top, left: The warthog has four large curved tusks and looks somewhat like a wild boar.

Bottom, left: The large-eared armadillo is well protected by the armor on his back.

Upper, right: This squirrel is a born explorer and spends his time nosing around in the woods for nuts, acorns, and pine cones.

Lower, right: The tapir who lives along the Amazon River is a distant cousin of the horse and the rhinoceros.

sticky and he flashes it out to catch ants, termites, and other insects. Once the anteater touches them with his sticky tongue, they cannot escape. He can extend his tongue about 21 inches. Think of it, my friends, that is pretty close to 2 full feet. The anteater's front paws have strong "fingers" and extremely powerful claws that serve as an excellent defense against his sworn enemies, the jaguar and the puma. Believe it or not, he often defeats these fierce and powerful animals in battle —an anteater's hug can mean death. The young travel for a long time on their mother's back, and if they are attacked, she defends them with great courage. Even the lesser anteater, or tamandua, has dangerous claws and is a fierce fighter.

The flying squirrel parachutes from branch to branch in jumps as long as 100 feet.
Left: A roe buck, a small, nimble and graceful deer.
Right: The adorable, teddy-bear-like koala bear who lives in Australia eats only the leaves of certain eucalyptus trees. The adult koala is about 2 feet long and weighs as much as 30 pounds.

WHERE IT IS A LITTLE COOLER

The plant life found in the forests of the temperate zones is not as rich as that in the tropical jungles we have just left. We find different kinds of trees in these forests—oaks, chestnuts, poplars, and beech trees. The animals that live in these forests are: deer, boar, squirrels, dormice, martens, wildcats, and lynx. Here in the temperate regions it is wise to keep a scarf handy, because it can be very cold. Oof, I put a rattlesnake around my neck instead of a scarf! He lives in these forests, too. What a mistake, though!

The animals we are visiting now have their own ways of keeping warm. Many of them make their homes underground. Others find good shelter in hollow tree trunks. The fox, badger, and groundhog, all burrow under the ground, while bears, for example, prefer a tree or even a dark cave. Otters dig into the river bank. The beaver, forever busy building dams, lives in a floating shelter. He has an under-

ground den for emergencies, with several of its entrances under the water. We'll leave him there and take a trip to another kind of forest.

IN THE SPICY PINE FOREST

A wide and impressive band of pine stretches from the mid-latitude forests to the northern tundra and covers a large area of the Northern Hemisphere. This kind of forest land is also known as the "taiga," the name given to it by the Russians. The mammals found in these forests are: deer, elk, rodents, wolves, bears, and lynx.

As long as we are here, let's stop and visit a bit with the lynx. The lynx lives in many of the forests of America, Asia, and parts of Europe. There are many kinds of lynx, but they all resemble one another. The color of their fur ranges from sand gray to a reddish brown spotted with black. In Europe, the lynx is also known as the deer wolf, and is slowly dying out. In Spain it is still possible to catch a glimpse of the leopard lynx, whose coat is yellow-brown with black spots. The lynx is an excellent climber and a daring

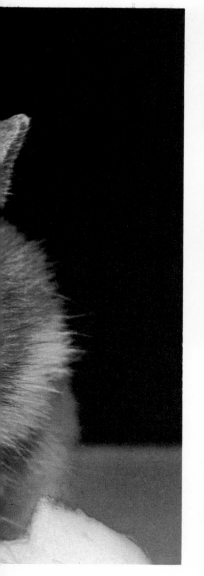

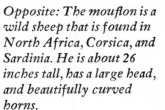

Center: The dormouse has but one worry and that is to keep his teeth in good shape. For this reason he eats continuously.
Above: Would you believe that this little American moose calf will grow up to be 6½ feet tall and weigh about half a ton? The American moose is found on the continent of North America and in Greenland.

Opposite: The mouflon is a wild sheep that is found in North Africa, Corsica, and Sardinia. He is about 26 inches tall, has a large head, and beautifully curved horns.

jumper, with a great weakness for a diet of birds. In fact, he could eat them for breakfast, lunch, and dinner. In Scandinavia and Siberia there is the Siberian lynx, and he is a real glutton, to say the least. He kills more prey than he can eat. The Siberian lynx has unusually wide paws, which serve him as "snowshoes." The large Canadian lynx also has big wide paws, and boasts a beautiful, soft, and silky coat. Because of it, he runs the constant risk of becoming some woman's fur coat! The red American lynx, or bobcat, has a thick coat also. He hunts rats. This is useful to us all, and since his coat

Black bears are not shy. They do not hesitate to walk up to a car full of tourists and beg for handouts, like these in Yellowstone National Park. In spite of their weight they are nimble, and when sensing danger, they climb a tree. They shinny up the tree, gripping the trunk with their forelegs and pushing themselves up by their hind legs. Once in the safety of the tree they nap.

Opposite: The grizzly bear would rather lie on solid ground than up in a tree.

is not considered of much value, he is left alone by man.

Here they are, boys and girls—the nicest citizens of the pine forest. They are the chipmunks, the hamsters, the squirrels, and the dormice—also known as golden mice or walnut mice because of the color of their coats and their favorite food.

The chipmunk, a member of the rodent family, is a charmer, with his soft coat of many colors. He has a small red and white face with two black stripes across it. His chest and belly are snow white, his tail is black and white, and his back is brown and black. He is unmistakable—and he sure is a chatterer.

Shhh! Don't wake the dormouse! This rodent, small, grey-brown and white, stores away enormous amounts of acorns and other nuts in the autumn, and then he goes to sleep for a long 6 months. When he finally wakes up, there is his food waiting for him.

THE BEARS—FRIENDLY, BUT WATCH OUT!

Let's go, fast, before that bear reaches out and swats us with his big paw. He sure can do it, so you'd better move on. Unless, of course, one of you happens to have a jar of honey handy? You have? Great! Then you do know how much bears love to eat honey. They simply go wild over it. So now that we have a jar of sweet honey, we can go ahead and arrange a meeting with the bears of the pine forest.

Let's begin with the huge grizzly bear, who is seldom found except in Canada and the Alaskan wilds. He can also be found in the national parks, where he is protected. He is a brownish yellow color, and is able to walk for miles. The

grizzly bear prefers to live close to a river. He has a very good reason for doing so. He is able to swim in the river and to fish for trout, which he very much likes to have for his dinner. Except for trout, and sometimes bees as a side dish, the grizzly lives off fruit, berries, and honey. Once greatly feared, this bear is a favorite today with the tourists in our national parks. But if you see him, keep your distance and admire him from afar.

Another favorite of the American continent is the black bear. Even though he is a good climber, runner, and swimmer, he doesn't give the appearance of being much of an athlete, for he is very unsteady on his feet. In fact, he isn't a sportsman at all, but just greedy. His favorite food is corn, but he will trespass on whatever land he can to steal a few ears off the

The polar bear is different from other bears because he lives in the far north where it is always cold, and he does not sleep through the winter.

stalk. He likes fish as well, and when it is time for the salmon to swim upstream as they do every year to give birth to their young, you'll find the black bear beside the rivers waiting for them. He loves his appetizers, too, and if he runs out of his supply of shellfish, or shrimp, he'll settle for a frog or two, some ants, or even termites.

Newborn bears are about the size of small rabbits. After 3 or 4 months, they will take their first steps, but are cared for by their mother for a whole year. After that, so it is said, it is their turn to look after baby sister and brother.

Well, boys and girls, our journey through the jungles and woods is over. The bear is napping, so I think we'll leave him and go on.

33

BEASTS OF THE OPEN COUNTRY

Here I am again. Your old friend Donald Duck and I have to admit that I feel more like a cat than ever! I've been planning a marvelous adventure for you. We'll let the wind blow us through prairies and deserts, over plains and tundra, and we will meet all the animals along the way, who live in these wide open spaces.

LET'S LOOK AROUND

The wide open spaces, whether plains, deserts, or steppes, have one thing in common: the absence, or partial absence, of trees, depending on the amount of moisture in the air and in the earth. We are going to see all of them, from the fairly damp areas—the plains of Africa, the Brazilian campos—to the North American prairies, the steppes of Central Asia, and the dry deserts and semi-deserts.

Let us take a look at the similarities among the animals living in these places and see how they have adapted to life there.

Sorry, friends. I get carried away by my interest in plants and animals. True, these subjects are not only important in themselves, but are also bound very closely with the lives of men and animals. But we must stick to our journey. And so I'll make it simple and say that the steppes and the plains have a great deal of grasses and bushes. Above all, there is a vast amount of space, where animals move in herds and flocks and where one can see for miles and miles.

The lion lives on the plains and the steppes, and so do the zebras and the antelopes. Of course. I say of course, because the zebras and the antelopes feed off the bushes and the grass; but the lions feed on the zebras and the antelopes.

CATS OF THE OPEN GRASSLANDS

Now boys and girls, we are going to join the animals of the open lands. Be careful, though, to move against the wind, so that the lion will not scent us. We are hoping to see him and have him wander away without knowing we're there. It would be too bad if all our travels ended now after all my trouble!

The lion. . . . How does he look? Since most of us have some idea of what the lion is like, let us start off with him. From the tip of his nose to the tuft at the end of his tail, he's about 10 feet long, and about 3 feet high, from his shoulder to the ground. He weighs between 325–500 pounds. Only the male has a mane, full around his head and falling down around his shoulders. It is about 1½ feet long. The lioness, except that she has no mane, is a slender copy of her mate. Their tails end in a fur tuft, under which is a sort of claw. When angry or irritated by flies, the lion whips his tail against his flanks. Our cats at home do the same thing, but because they are perhaps more clever, they merely give their tails a flick. Like our cats, too, the lion will nibble on grass when his insides are out of order. But he is carnivorous (meat-eating) and his favorite food is meat, raw, and preferably fresh—the flesh of some beast he has killed that day. During most of the daytime, the lion lies in the shade of some tree or rolls on the grass with his fellows. It is only when night falls that the swift and silent lion hunts. He is always careful to move up wind and so is able to surprise the zebra, gazelle, buffalo, and other animals who are his victims. Unlike the tiger, leopard, and similar cats, the lion kills only for food and never for the sport of killing itself. It is always the male who eats first. When he has had his fill, the lioness and cubs have their turn.

What's left is put aside in a special place, for the next day. Once he has eaten, and is satisfied, the lion is relatively harmless. He doesn't even take the trouble to

swat at a lamb, should it walk under his nose. In the home of the lion, it is the lioness who rules. She is a terror and can make a lot of trouble, especially when her cubs are around. Her mate, poor fellow, must stay clear of his children until they are several weeks old. Then with permission and under the stern and protective eye of the lioness, he is allowed to play a little with his cubs. Always, of course, if there is no "tiger horse" in sight.

Opposite: Lions are sociable creatures who like to live in families rather than in herds as other animals do. The families are usually made up of from 6 to 20 animals. The lionesses are good to all the young and often nurse cubs belonging to other mothers. The cubs stay with their mothers for about 2 years, that is, until they have learned the art of hunting and killing their prey without risking a kick in the face from a zebra. Above, right: The zebra's only defenses are his hooves, speed, good sense of smell, and good eyesight.

Above: Gliding silently over the plains, the leopard sneaks up unseen on his prey. Leopards are sly, fierce fighters. They eat many different animals—cattle, sheep, antelopes, monkeys, dogs, and birds.

Left: One creature the leopard cannot count on is the maned porcupine. When he senses danger, this spiky mammal curls himself into a ball, with all his quills pointed, and waits for better times. The maned porcupine lives in Sicily, in the Balkans, and in northern and eastern Africa.

Right: Cheetahs are found in parts of eastern Africa and in southern Asia. Their long bodies and slender legs help them run short distances faster than any other animal.

Far right: The fennec, or desert fox, has unusually large ears that allow him to hear the slightest noise.

"Tiger horse," you ask? Don't be puzzled. This is just an old name for the zebra. This animal, like his enemy, the lion, likes the wide open spaces where he can run and kick and play with other zebras. You may think that all zebras look alike. This is not the case at all, for the color of their stripes varies considerably—from a very light pink shade to brown, off-white, dark yellow and black stripes of differing widths. Zebras like to be with each other and gather in herds of 10 to 12 or else mingle in herds of other animals

such as wildebeest or even ostriches.

One of the main concerns of the zebra is the getting of water, for this can be a dangerous matter for our striped friend. Almost every time he goes down to the waterhole, his enemy the lion is sitting there waiting for him. So, you can see it's really not an easy thing living the life of a zebra.

Hey, watch out! Here come the cheetahs, racing by at full speed. Since these cats sprint at 65 miles an hour with ease, you will feel quite a big draft as he rushes

by. The cheetah is one of the swiftest runners on earth. He isn't much of an eater, in fact quite the opposite, since he can go for days between one meal and the next. When he does eat, he likes the smaller antelopes and similiar prey for his dinner. He has long legs and stands at the shoulder some 3½ feet high. The cheetah weighs as much as 145 pounds. He is a fairly quiet animal, doesn't roar like a lion, nor does he have the deep voice of his cousin the tiger. When he is in a good mood he sometimes purrs like a happy housecat.

Cheetahs love their family dearly, and in spite of their race into the distance, they always remember to come home. During their "cubhood" cheetahs are not very sure of themselves, and stay quite close to their mothers for about 2 years. You can be sure there is no rebellion in the family. The cheetah, even as a cub, is gentle and affectionate. It is a pity that man likes this animal's fur more than his easy nature and so hunts him down.

39

THE THIRSTY DESERT

How strange! It seems to me that we are in the desert. I bet we arrived here chasing after a cheetah. I didn't plan to be here just yet, but since we are, I'll introduce you to the fennec. He looks sleepy, doesn't he? And I doubt that he knows we're here. The fennec sleeps all day long. What is he? Why, the desert fox, of course. His ears are enormous in proportion to the rest of him, and they allow him to hear the slightest noise. At the sound of anything threatening he digs furiously into the ground to hide.

The hyena (above) and the jackal (below) hunt in groups that often include lions (left). The hyenas and jackals live on the lions' leftovers.

His legs kick so rapidly that an onlooker would find it hard to tell which leg is moving. As I told you, he sleeps all day. When he wakes up at night, he has a drink and then he goes on the hunt, mainly for lizards and rodents. If after a while he can't find what he wants, he settles for a lighter snack, such as birds' eggs or dates. Now, let's take a good look at this animal, whose tail, body, and head together do not measure more than 1 ½ feet. His ears are as wide and as long as his entire head. It is really thanks to his smallness, though, that the fennec can survive in such an unfriendly surrounding.

The desert where the fennec lives, contains snakes and insects all able to live in the hottest of climates with very little water. Desert mammals don't require much water. Like rodents, they do not sweat a great deal. Their bodies have ways of allowing them to store the water they drink. Many antelopes and armadillos are able to survive for a long time without drinking a drop. They satisfy their thirst with the liquid that is in the plants and animals they eat.

41

*The American badger, or carcajou,
uses his short legs to dig his den.*

Both the camel and the dromedary are able to go for long periods without water. But when these fellows do drink, they sure put a lot of liquid into their bodies. They like fresh water, but if that is not around, they'll drink seawater, and you know how salty that can be!

AGAINST THE DESERT HEAT AND COLD

Quick temperature changes are often found in the open plains. This is the case not only from season to season, but often from day to night as well. For example, in Africa a 40-degree change in temperature in one day is very possible. Freezing temperatures are not uncommon in the Sahara.

In such conditions, life on the land's surface for cold-blooded animals becomes a difficult business. I want to point out, friends, that the body temperature of cold-blooded animals, such as fish, frogs, and snakes goes up and down depending on the outside temperature. Warm-blooded animals keep more or less the same temperature within their bodies. But even warm-blooded animals must find a way of protecting themselves agains sudden and sharp temperature changes.

One good way to survive under such hardship is to live underground, in tunnels or holes dug into earth or sand. At about 1½ feet below the surface, it is cooler in summer and warmer in winter. And so the desert animals, rodents chiefly, live underground—especially in daytime. Typical of these below-ground rodents is the prairie dog, found in North America, and the Alpine pika or whistling hare of the Mongolian steppes in Asia. Pikas are farsighted. They plan ahead, digging holes and using them to store the hay and herbs which are their favorite food.

Many mammals, because they live in this sort of environment, have greatly developed endurance and speed. Because these animals must cover long distances in order to reach water and must be ready for quick escape from their enemies, they have become excellent runners and marvelous jumpers.

I can't tell you if I would jump or run if I were being chased by a cheetah, or even by the slower lion. After all, we ducks are somewhat handicapped. I only know that I'd do my very best to save myself, and keep all of my feathers.

42

Let's return to the matter of sports. Some animals prefer to leap rather than run, and can go faster this way. The best-known of this type of animal is the Australian kangaroo. He can cover as much as 30 feet in one leap. Many rodents in different parts of the world have a similar body structure, that is, their rear legs and tail (which they use to lean on and to keep their balance) are highly developed. With the exceptions of South America and Europe, there are jumping mice all over the world: in Africa, Asia, Australia, and North America.

FRIENDLY ALLIES

On the open plains you can see for long distances, and nearly all the inhabitants have excellent eyesight and hearing. It is, above all, the sense of sight that is so very, very important, friends, when it

A curious battle takes place between the rattlesnake and the kangaroo mouse. As soon as he sees his enemy, the mouse jumps straight up in the air. He watches and waits for the snake to attack. When the snake flicks his tongue, the mouse uses his four paws to throw sand at the snake.

comes to seeking food or spotting your enemies. Some animals like to collect in large groups. This is so among the animals of the open plains, such as the antelopes, the buffaloes, the zebras, and the guanacos. Many times a herd may be made up of more than one kind of animal. The hemionos of Central Asia are nearly always found in the company of wild sheep. The Tibetan antelope and the yak are usually together. Hyenas and jackals hunt in groups, sometimes even with the fierce and hungry lion. Now, the giraffe. . . .

I think we'll stop a moment and talk at greater length about the giraffe. First of all, since we were on that subject before, I want to tell you that giraffes too live in groups with other animals such as zebras, various kinds of antelopes, gazelles, and ostriches.

A giraffe has a long neck—a very long neck. Altogether giraffes are about 16 to 18 feet tall. Because of their height and their exceptionally good eyesight, they serve as lookouts for the rest of the herd. They can spot an enemy a long way off. In spite of their shyness and peace-loving disposition, they are well able to defend themselves against the big cats who every now and then attempt to attack them. Their big hooves are deadly and a lion who has tangled with them once will seldom try it again. Completely peaceful, the giraffes live in groups. The leader is the only one allowed to cut in front of another giraffe when the group is traveling along. Speaking of the giraffe, I must tell you that he has a heart as big as all outdoors, as they say. In actual fact, the heart of this animal weighs more than 23 pounds and is able to pump about 51½ quarts of blood a minute. You must understand, my friends, that this force is necessary to pump the blood all the way

44

Peccaries are small piglike animals found in North and South America. They are sociable animals and live and travel in bands.

up that long neck until it reaches the brain. Too quick a rush of blood to the head, though, might cause a lot of trouble up there in the brain and kill the poor fellow. And so when the giraffe bends his neck down to drink, his circulation is regulated by special valves. As soon as the giraffe lowers his head below his body, the safety valves close and prevent the flow of blood to the brain.

On the subject of the giraffe and eating: this fellow's long neck enables him to eat leaves that are beyond the reach of other ground-dwelling animals. Let's close with this bit of information—Arabs call the giraffe "zarafah," that is, "nice creature who walks with a sure tread."

This description of a sure and graceful step certainly cannot be applied to the

Rhinoceroses have very large, heavy bodies and usually move very slowly. But if they become angry, they can charge at speeds of about 30 miles an hour. Rhinoceroses do not hunt other animals for food. They eat only grass and other plants. They are the only animals not afraid of fire. Instead of running off in fright or steering clear of it, a campfire may make a rhinoceros angry and he may even attack.

rhinoceros. Even the eyesight of this powerful animal isn't very good. To make up for this, boys and girls, nature has given him a thick skin! The people of the region hunt the rhinoceros for this thick skin. After killing the animal, they manage to remove the skin and make shields from it. The shields are so tough that not even a strong lance can penetrate them. Perhaps we'd better talk about these dangerous animals right now and get it over with so that we can pass on to the rest undisturbed!

Both the black and the white African rhinos have two horns. One horn of the black rhino measures over 2 feet; the other over 1 foot. The horns of the white rhino measure 4 feet and 2 feet. The Sumatra rhino also has two horns. One is 2 feet long; the other less than a foot. The Indian rhino has only one horn, measuring 2 feet. All horns, whether big, medium, or small, are used by rhinos to gore their enemies. Let's stay clear of this beast and move on. We have a good chance, because as I have already told you, his eyesight is pretty poor. But be careful that he doesn't hear you, because his hearing is excellent. To show off for his relatives the tapir and the horse, the rhino trots about on his funny but agile hooves. The rhino's skin, in spite of its thickness, is very sensitive to insect bites. To rid himself of insects, the animal soaks himself in a pond or stream. When he is not able to reach water he keeps a layer of mud on his skin. When this mud dries, it forms a protective covering. The most

45

persistent of the insects are disposed of by the bufagas, birds that will eat almost anything. These birds perch on the rhino's broad back and just eat away. And the rhinos don't seem to mind having the bufagas around. In fact, they seem to be completely delighted.

Friends, you'll be thinking that Donald has a weakness for rhinos, because I've gone on so long about them. The truth is I'm trying to be fair to all my new friends.

African buffalo are also called black buffalo because of their color. Wild and untamable, this buffalo fears only the lion, which he sometimes succeeds in striking and killing. In the two photographs below: antelope. There are so many types of antelope and gazelle and they run in such large herds, that it is difficult even for specialists to distinguish each individual type within the numerous families.

PLAYING DEAD—TO STAY ALIVE

There's only one way to behave if you're around the African buffalo, and that is to play dead. I mean if you shot at

the animal and missed him. Really, it is the buffalo who plays dead to survive. This happens when the buffalo, alive after a hunter's near miss, realizes that there will be another shot coming. The animal drops to the ground. The hunters, of course, believe that he is really dead and approach to admire their prey—when all of a sudden. . . . You can take my word for it, if those hunters don't get away fast, it's the end for them.

THE WONDERFUL STEPPES

I wish it were otherwise, but having to talk now about the steppes makes me feel completely helpless. So I asked for reliable information from someone else. I've called on Ludwig von Drake. He was in good form and talked for 24 hours on end. Here I am, tired but happy, and ready to pass it all on to you.

The steppes—what a magic sound it has! And to think that all it is, is grass, green in the rainy season, and yellow and arid in the dry season. This sort of land is known as prairie in North America, pampas in Argentina, puszta in Hungary, lande in France, and steppes in southeastern Europe and Asia.

The Eurasian steppes are vast, stretching from Hungary and southern Russia across all of central Asia. There is a similar kind of land, though on a smaller scale, in South Africa, Australia, and Chile.

Top, left: Two surprised and alarmed prairie dogs. These rodents are tireless diggers and their tunnels are often as deep as 16 feet.
Left: The mará or Patagonian hare.
Opposite above: These single humped camels, are ownerless and unbranded. They roam freely over the deserts of Arabia, North Africa, and the Middle East.

48

In the dry earth of this vast region there lives a strange rodent that is something like a hare, but which actually is a close relative of the guinea pig. He is called the mará, or Patagonian hare. During the day this animal remains hidden in a deep underground dwelling, but at night he's up and about. He comes up to graze with friends and relatives—and even in the smallest spaces, they munch together on grass roots and stems. The mará's hind legs are long, so he is a high jumper. Unfortunately, the mará for some reason or other—maybe it's his high jumping—attracts too many hunters for his own good.

After 1900, when poachers in Yellowstone National Park killed sixteen of the remaining 20 head of bison, naturalists believed that the American bison was doomed to die out. Only a few decades earlier, thousands and thousands of bison had roamed free over the prairies. When the West was won, bison were killed by the thousand. But when it became known that only four had survived, many zoos sent their bison to join the survivors so that the species wouldn't die out. Today there are about 30,000 living bison. A typical South American animal is the llama, photographed below. Notice the long neck, small size, and absence of hump, even though this animal is related to the camel. The llama can carry loads of up to 100 lbs. at altitudes no other animal would survive.

On the steppes, animal life depends directly upon plant life. Every bit of a plant is used for food, from the roots to the tips of blades of grass. Since the bushes are sometimes thorny and very tough, obviously good chewing ability is needed. Rodents and ungulates (horses, antelopes, and buffaloes—animals with hooves) have sharp front teeth that enable the animal to cut leaves and branches. These animals also have very strong molars for chewing food.

The problem of water is partly solved by the use of such plants as cactus—which provide both food and water at the same time. But should the last water hole dry up, the animals of the steppes must move away.

When the land is covered with snow there are other problems of survival. One of the problems is how to resist the cold. The animals that suffer the least are the larger mammals with thick fur and a reserve of fat. The buffalo, the yak, and wild camel can even afford to play in the snow. But other animals are forced to migrate. Antelopes and wild donkeys leave the Gobi Desert in Asia not because of snow, but because the water freezes over. The trails made by bison across the North American plains during their winter travels were once famous.

Let's talk a little about this fine big beast who is the North American buffalo. Come with me to Yellowstone National Park in the United States, where at last the buffalo is able to live in complete peace, protected and almost spoiled by those whose job it is to look after them. What do the keepers do? Simple: when the temperature drops below zero and when the white snow is piled very high in big drifts, the keepers deliver hay by the ton to every buffalo.

Now it seems to me that the snow here has covered everything with a white blanket. Pay special attention to the following tracks. Yes, I said tracks.

FOOTPRINTS WE CAN FOLLOW

All of the bears are members of the family that is called Ursidae. When they walk they place their weight on the soles of their feet. Thanks to this large "support" area, they are able to walk erect.

The paws of bears have five fingers, with long, heavy nonretractable claws. The polar bear's fingers are joined at the base by a membrane that facilitates swimming. The Canidae, or dog family, use only the toes of their paws to walk on. These toes, five to the forepaws and four to the hindpaws, have rather straight nonretractable claws. Insectivorous animals (those who

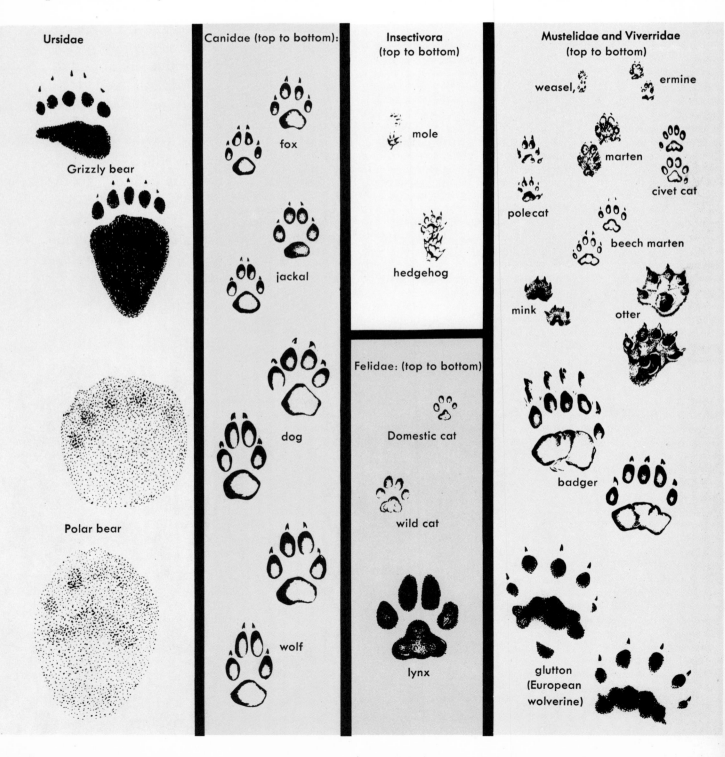

Ursidae

Grizzly bear

Polar bear

Canidae (top to bottom):

fox

jackal

dog

wolf

Insectivora (top to bottom)

mole

hedgehog

Felidae: (top to bottom)

Domestic cat

wild cat

lynx

Mustelidae and Viverridae (top to bottom)

weasel,

ermine

marten

civet cat

polecat

beech marten

mink

otter

badger

glutton (European wolverine)

feed on insects) have short, five-fingered paws facing outward to make it easy to dig and remove earth. The Felidae, the cat family, have large, almost chubby five-fingered paws on the front legs and four-fingered paws on the hind legs. The nails are thin and retractable (can be drawn in). The mustelines have small paws with four or five fingers and retractable nails. Viverines are civets and similar to mustelines. Ungulates are hooved animals. Rodents in general have very strong paws with sharp, curved nails. Hunters are easily able to distinguish the many different paw prints. They can do this not because they love science and have studied the paw prints, but because they love furs.

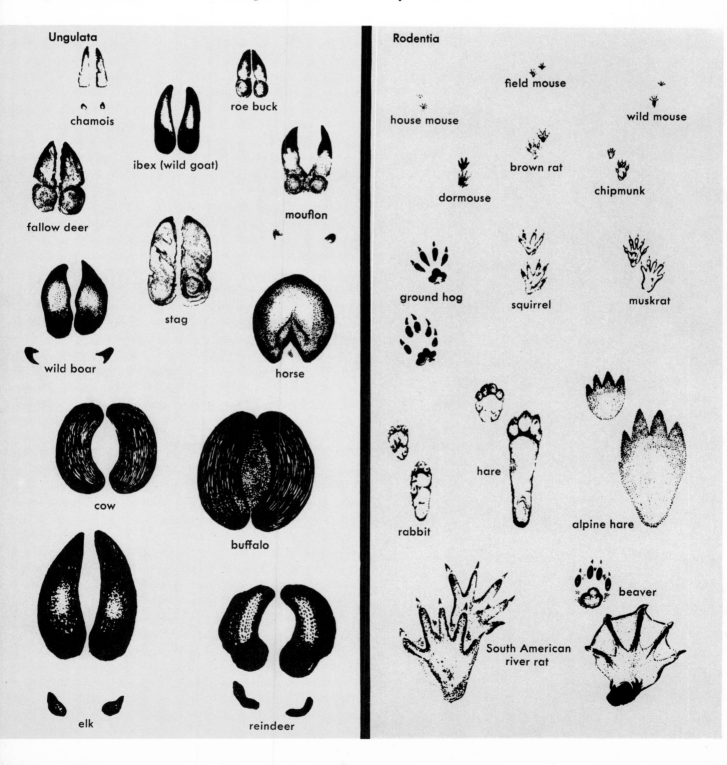

Ungulata

chamois

roe buck

ibex (wild goat)

mouflon

fallow deer

stag

horse

wild boar

cow

buffalo

elk

reindeer

Rodentia

field mouse

house mouse

wild mouse

dormouse

brown rat

chipmunk

ground hog

squirrel

muskrat

rabbit

hare

alpine hare

South American river rat

beaver

DRESSED TO MATCH THEIR SURROUNDINGS

Boys and girls, I've thought up a trip that would be the envy of the hardest-working travel agent. Are you with me? This is what I've planned: we'll explore regions where no one goes except by mistake. We'll tour the swamps. I'll show you the tundra, those treeless plains of the Arctic. We'll look at the shores of rivers, lakes, and seas. I have something for everyone, whatever his tastes.

Let us begin by taking a careful look at the environment. Animals who live in swamps and along shores have an abundance of water. There is also always plenty of food, and it is so tasty that it attracts large numbers of animals. Naturally, a good many of these animals know how to swim. It surely would be tragic for them if they didn't, wouldn't it, boys and girls!

For many of the animals, there are, in addition to the the plants that grow in the water, huge numbers of insects to eat. In the summer, the tundras of North America and Asia are blackened by gnats, mosquitoes, horseflies, and sandflies. These insects are a real threat to the unlucky traveler who has come without an insect repellent!

For some animals the water serves as a refuge from the heat. Other animals use the water as a place to escape from their land-based enemies. The water is also the hunting preserve of many animals. It is interesting to see how various animals are fitted, or *adapted*, for seeking their food in the water. For example, the frog, the crocodile, and the hippopotamus all have nostrils that they can close underwater. Their eyes, too, are fitted for seeing underwater, where they can remain for several minutes at a time. The hippopotamus, a vegetarian, can move about the river bottom, finding the grasses on which it feeds. It spends much of its time floating at the surface, with only its ears, eyes, and nostrils showing above the water.

Frogs and crocodiles, both meat-eaters, may also be seen floating with only eyes and nostrils showing above water. They wait for their prey to come close, then suddenly come to life, catching their victim in a flash.

One of the most interesting animals of this type is the Australian platypus, the only mammal with a duck's bill. I'm going to tell you more about the platypus later on. So just be patient.

There are many animals who live around rivers, lakes, and swamps: the beaver, nutria, otter, and muskrat. This small fellow, the muskrat, was originally from North America. Prized for its fur, it was introduced in Europe around 1905. Today the muskrat can be found all the way from France to Kamchatka in Russia.

In Western Europe, for example,

where the muskrat digs deep burrows along river banks and at the edges of dams, he is looked upon as a pest who causes damage. This is particularly so when we remember that the muskrat is always active, day and night. But there are regions where he is hunted for his fur, and therefore in those places he does have value as a source of income.

But let me add, boys and girls, that among other animals of the coastal regions are seals and otters. Although these mammals are usually found in the sea, they seek dry land only to give birth to their young. I'll have more to tell you about seals and otters when we reach the polar regions. So, if you have any questions about these lovely animals, hold them awhile. Thanks.

Along the river banks you'll find the ungulates—those mammals with hooves—such as tapirs, many kinds of antelopes, reindeer, elk, caribou, and Asian buffalo. Most of these are herbivorous animals—they do not eat meat.

THE WATER LORDS

Now, let's talk about one of the most interesting of all animals. That's right, I'm talking about the hippopotamus.

The strange-looking duckbill platypus lives in Australia and Tasmania and has a flat tail similar to the beaver's and very short legs. His body is shaped like a sausage and his 'hands' and 'feet' are enormous, with five fingers each and strong claws. His hind paws have 'palms' right up to the base of his nails, and on the front paws the membrane covers the nails (see photo at right). His head is most unusual with no ears. His hearing ducts and eyes are closed by wrinkles in the skin. His mouth is shaped like a duck's bill and is as flexible as rubber.

You may not know it, but there was a time when the hippopotamus lived undisturbed in the swamps of Africa—particularly in the Congo.

But little by little, as trees were cut down and large areas put into cultivation, the hippo and man found themselves lined up against each other. For example, during the night the hippos would invade the fields looking for juicy roots and other things to eat. How could the hippos be kept out? Man decided the only way was to destroy the hippopotamus.

This uneven battle went on for a while, with the hippo losing out quite badly. But then another problem arose that was much more serious to man. This problem was known by the poetic name of "water lily." This ordinary floating plant happened to be one of the hippopotamus' favorite dishes. When there were very few hippos left to eat the water lilies, these plants began to grow and grow. They grew so fast they began to clog the water of lakes and rivers of Africa. The rivers were so clogged that it was almost impossible to get a boat through. So it was decided to start bring-

57

The capybara is the largest living rodent, weighing up to 200 lbs. The one shown above is a cub. The Indian buffalo (below) is an excellent beast of burden in marshy regions.

ing the hippos back into the very same regions from which they had been driven.

The water lily has been found to be actually dangerous to man. The water lily makes possible the reproduction of certain water snails. These water snails carry a worm that causes a sickness in man.

DRUMBEAT OF THE BUSY BEAVER

Many mammals that live in swamps have flat tails. This tail looks very strange, but it is very useful to its owner in swimming and also helps him when he must make an escape. Let's take the beaver. I

Above: It's no secret that the otter would rather live in water than on land. He can stay underwater for great lengths of time and when he surfaces, he barely sticks his nose out. He isn't bothered by cold and he is a very playful clown. Right: A close-up of the hippopotamus, his eyes sticking up out of the water like a periscope. Below: A group of hippos standing on a tiny islet.

knew one once—I met him in Montana—
and he owned a 2,000 foot dam (this size
dam must have beaten the record!).
Well, this beaver's tail was long, flat, and
scaly. He told me, my friend in Montana,
that he uses it for steering when he swims,
as a prop when he sits, and for defense. I
don't mean that the beaver uses his tail

60

*The beaver has fascinated man since very early
times and has influenced our life in many ways.
Building his dams, the beaver has created ponds,
which after many thousands of years form
immense pastures and fertile plains. The two lower
photographs on the opposite page show the
shape of the beaver's paw and tail. Opposite, top:
There is the velvet-antlered caribou, a close
relative of the reindeer, though not the same size.*

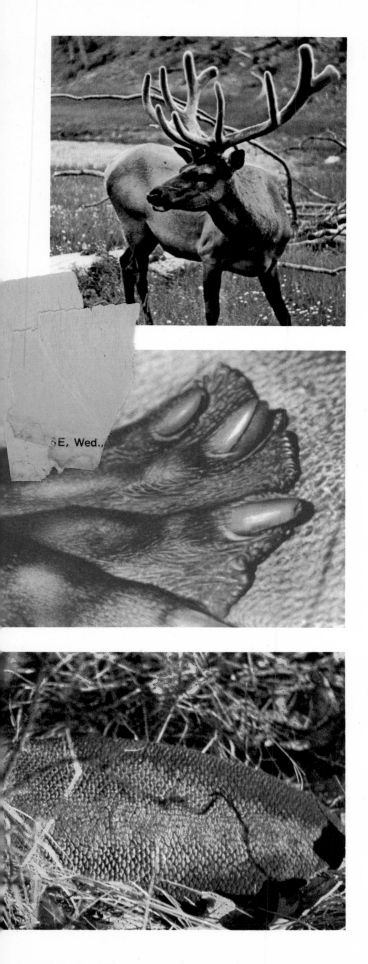

when he's attacked to slap his enemy around. He does use it to slap the water like a drum major. The sound serves as an order for his companions, all busy at work building houses, to dive beneath the surface. In fact, the beavers obey the drumming. They drop their work instantly and dive to safety.

However, in spite of this organized warning system, the beaver, once very common, almost disappeared from the face of the earth. This was due to man's handiwork, for he had discovered just how soft and valuable the beaver's fur could be. Matters have improved somewhat. In North America, the beaver has a more peaceful life than he had in the past, because we have learned that such slaughter of animals can only hurt us in the long run. In Norway, France, and in the Rhone valley of Germany, our friend the beaver lives proudly and happily protected by laws.

A SMALL HOME OF BRANCHES

When he has picked the spot he likes along the river banks, the beaver faces the problem of building his "home sweet home." The intelligent, hard-working beaver always wants his house to be useful and very safe. When it's time for work to begin, the beavers vanish into the deep woods. There they collect and prepare the necessary raw materials. Each beaver, with the help of his four strong, sharp front teeth, cuts down trees, breaks the branches, and strips the bark. Not only do they strip the bark, they eat it as well, since it is their main diet.

Then, using all his strength in a sort of assembly line operation, each beaver carries a tree trunk or branch to the building site where the other beavers wait, to carry on with the construction itself. With the skill and experience of an engineer, and the imagination of an architect, these beavers make sure that each part of the house suits the purpose it is meant to serve. The living room is always above water level, while the entrance—a tunnel about 15 to 20 feet long—begins underwater. There is also a service entrance—a larger tunnel than the first—through which twigs, bark, and roots are carried and stored away.

Although part of the house is underwater, it is perfectly dry, because Father beaver has put down a sort of mat at the front entrance. Here the beavers dry their feet and shake their fur out—down to the last drop of water. The water drips from this mat to the ground beneath it. The living room stays dry and really is a snug place. When the house is finished the beavers check the dams—which were built beforehand—to make sure they are still in good condition and won't flood.

A WELL-PROTECTED NEST

The platypus, too, is a clever builder. He is by nature a complicated fellow, and so his den couldn't be anything else but very complicated indeed. Some dens are living quarters for the whole family. Others are reserved for the females to lay their eggs and raise their children. This section is built near the water, with many entrances hidden near the roots of nearby trees. The other sections are really long tunnels with surfaces just above water level. The house has two entrances that lead to the "nursery." Mother platypus won't leave it though, until she's finished nursing her little ones.

HUNTED BUT HAPPY

Isn't the Big Bad Wolf going to go to sleep for the whole winter? I guess not. Instead he's gone a little crazy and looks as though he'd rather hunt a lonely duck than the Three Little Pigs, or even three little raccoons. Ah well, let's take a look at the raccoons, who may have eaten your corn this summer, if you were growing any.

This native of areas that lie around the swamps and creeks is very intelligent and very friendly. He has a funny little face with a sort of mask over it. Just look at the picture on the opposite page, and you'll see what I mean. The raccoon is very vulnerable indeed, because his fur is so beautiful to look at, and is quite warm, too. This means that he is much hunted by man. He spends a good part of his time running and hiding from hunters and their dogs. Man also makes the life of a raccoon miserable by setting traps for him. Even so, the raccoon is a playful fellow and just loves to eat—always trying to get as much food as he can between his skillful paws.

Raccoons are often seen roaming about the areas of swamps. They also search for food along the banks of streams. Raccoons eat frogs, shrimps, and other shellfish, and vary their diet with corn—ah, how they love sweet corn. They also like eggs, fruit, meat, and nuts. Raccoons are very clean about their food. That's right. They wash their food before popping it into their mouths—this is, of course, if they happen to be near a stream.

Although, as I told you, the raccoon is a playful fellow and pretty gentle, he can be a very tough fighter when cornered. So, don't tangle with him!

AMONG THE MOSS AND LICHEN

Right now, why don't we go for a breath of air in the tundra? What did you say? You don't feel like it? Well, friends, if you think that after I've read up on all

Left: A trio of appealing raccoons. They are usually wild and aggressive animals. When frightened, the raccoon lets out very strange sounds indeed, something like a long whistle, but so high-pitched it's almost inaudible to the human ear. The raccoon can make an excellent house pet. Right: A graceful and alert ermine. He has a reddish-brown coat during the summer. In the winter the ermine is all white except for the dark tip of his tail. The ermine's fur is characteristically soft and shiny. He belongs to the Mustelidae family. Skunks, minks, and martens are also among the Mustelidae. All of these animals are small and carnivorous. Their fur is highly valued by man.

Left: A badger comes to a pond to drink. He is a beautiful specimen. The dens of badgers are clean and neat. Above: An elk, cropping grass. Below: A graceful Canadian deer stands in a clearing of the woods. He is ever alert to the presence of danger and ever ready to turn and dash away into the cover of the trees. Bottom, right: An otter in the winter snow. Note his paws with their webbed membranes. The membranes are useful in swimming.

the moss and lichen that grow in the tundra I'm going to pass it by, you're just wrong!

So—the tundra is land covered by dwarf plants, like moss and lichen. Sometimes all of it is covered by snow and ice. The tundra regions are: the Yenisei basin (the Yenisei is a Siberian river flowing into the Arctic Sea); the coastal areas and the islands that face the Bering Sea; Greenland; the region around Hudson Bay; and the islands surrounding the Arctic pole.

Why is it that moss and lichen alone grow in these parts? Well, because the soil just beneath the earth's surface is nearly always frozen and no other vegetation can grow because it cannot put down deep roots. The tundra covers the Arctic regions of the Northern Hemisphere where living conditions are severe in winter. Generally, it is the warm-blooded animals like birds and mammals who are better able to live there all year round. Warm-blooded animals have a constant body temperature no matter how warm or cold the place they live in. Small animals such as the lemming, fox, and Arctic hare are protected against the

cold by a sort of double fur. The layer closest to the skin is very thick and wooly. The coat of the musk ox is made up of long fur, which gives him a protec- tive covering right down to his paws. He also has a thick layer of fat, which keeps in his body heat. In similar fashion, the Arc- tic hare becomes very fat when winter comes. In contrast, his brother, the European hare, who is not exposed to such great cold, remains lean throughout the year.

Some birds and mammals living in the Arctic tundra fit themselves to the change in their surroundings by turning white during the winter. This change of color helps the animals to blend in with their surroundings until they are almost invisible to their enemies. The ermine, the fox, and the Arctic hare are champion artists of the quick change. In fact, the ermine's fur, which during the warmer weather stays a reddish brown, becomes thick and white in winter time. Poor fellow, the tip of his tail remains dark, and so he can still be spotted by his enemies, and so often loses his whole coat and his life!

The tundra reindeer and his American neighbor, the caribou, are perhaps the only cud-chewing animals who are completely at home in the polar regions. They lumber around after the Lapps. Actually, the Lapp shepherds, those who live in the mountain regions, are nomads.

We might call the reindeer "queen of the tundra," since her kingdom is so enormous. This wandering animal lives in the vast territories that surround the North Pole: Canada, Alaska, Greenland, Lapland, and Siberia. The reindeer eats mostly lichen or reindeer moss, wild mushrooms, and willow leaves.

They follow the reindeer herds that are constantly searching for pasture. The reindeer are always on the lookout for northern lichen, also called reindeer moss, which the animals dig out with their sharp hooves. If this moss cannot be found, the reindeer will eat wild mushrooms and willow leaves. When the animal is successful in the search for food, the Lapp is happy, for to him the reindeer is everything. The reindeer's fur is used for mattresses; his skin for jackets, gloves, and pants; his nerves for thread to sew together the sealskin canoe (the thread expands in the water, and the seams become waterproofed).

So let's catch the first sleigh that comes along and go . . . where? You'll see when we turn the page.

A MOUNTAIN PEAK IS HOME

Whoever loves me will follow me! Clear the way! Hey, I'm talking to you, boys and girls. Sorry if I've changed the subject abruptly, but you can understand my position. If I loosen my grip, goodbye. Oh, I forgot . . . see how confused I am. If you want to come with me, grab hold of one of these antennas . . . I mean antlers. You can trust him; he is the bold, daring, and acrobatic ibex. Hold on tight now.

An ibex is a wild goat who likes to roam the mountains of Europe and Asia. He's taking us up very high, isn't he? He certainly is a sure-footed animal, and he climbs with such ease. Now he is letting us down and going off on his own. So, let's see where we are now.

There: what we are looking at down below us is "Alpine meadow." But don't think that because I said Alpine it means we are in the Alps. All regions above the altitude where trees grow are known as Alpine—all over the world. Above the Alpine meadow begins the kingdom of eternal snow and glaciers. Below the Alpine meadow where trees and forests grow, the animal life is similar to that found in the wooded areas of the plains. The strip of land dividing the tree growing region from that of perpetual ice and snow can in turn be divided into two zones: a bush zone and a zone with some grass but little other vegetation.

This subdivision holds true only in the highest mountain ranges. But we must remember that the limits of the tree line depend upon latitude, upon the direction which the mountain slope faces, north or south, and upon the type of climate.

In the Andes Mountains of Colombia, South America, the forests begin to grow at 9,000 feet above sea level. This is quite unlike the growth found in the Arctic regions of Norway. There, beyond the polar areas, the forest zone begins at 800 feet or so above sea level.

What makes an Alpine zone different from the lower regions? For one thing, at higher altitudes, the air pressure, or atmospheric pressure, is lower. Temperatures are lower, too, and there is an increase in the humidity of the air.

Different animals react differently to lowered air pressure. For example, a man or a monkey begins to suffer from lowered air pressure long before a frog does.

Oh, dear, sorry about that scientific stuff, but I thought you needed to catch your breath. This matter of altitude and pressure is really quite a headache, but the idea is not too hard to understand. To

71

The ibex, or wild goat (capra hibex) is an ancient animal. It is said that it originated in the Caucasus (in the south of Russia) and arrived on the Alps some million years ago. Once lord of high European peaks, today the ibex is forced to live in a herd of a few thousand among the crags and glaciers of the Gran Paradiso National Park (in northern Italy), and in some regions of Switzerland and Austria.

June

September

January

THE GROWTH OF ANTLERS

Among animals belonging to the deer family, adult males are recognized by horns that become great antlers, which grow like branches of a tree. In the white-tailed deer, they reach maximum growth by the November mating season. During this time, the male sheds the velvety covering of his antlers. The antlers provide the animal with a sharp weapon that he can use against his rivals.

2 years

6 years

12 years

THE GROWTH OF HORNS

The Rocky Mountain sheep, is one of the wild sheep in the United States today. The horns are big: up to 1½ feet in the adult—the reason the animal is also known as "Big Horn". These horns appear at eight weeks, and look like hard little buttons. They grow rapidly during the second year, and every year after that a growth ring is added. In the other older rams, the tips of the horns curve back.

help you catch on, I waylaid Ludwig von Drake by his coattail one day (he was in a hurry and didn't want to help) and now I'm passing on to you what he told me.

Air is thickest, or most dense, at sea level and at low altitudes. As we go up a mountainside, the air gets thinner and thinner. Because all living things need the oxygen that air contains, there is less life found in the higher places of the earth. When men try to reach a towering mountain peak they must carry a supply of oxygen with them. The climbers of Mount Everest (29,028 feet above sea level) carried an artificial oxygen tank as a necessary part of their pack. Others have been able to climb 27,000 feet with-

out this aid. In Tibet and the Andes the highest permanent colony of man is at 17,000 feet. Shepherds and their flocks, however, frequently go as high as 18,000 feet. Mammals such as wild sheep and goats, yaks, hares, and wolves live at high altitudes on the Asian mountains quite comfortably. The takin, too, which is a strange Tibetan antelope, lives on the high mountain peaks.

What's that, my friend? You want to know what sort of animal this takin is? Let me tell you. He's a budorca. The budorca, or takin, is a cud-chewing animal living in the Himalayas who roams around a backyard some 6,500 feet to 16,000 feet in height. He doesn't suffer 73

Left: A gray squirrel. This excellent climber builds his nest high up in trees, storing his nuts in the hollow trunks. Above: A young fox standing over his fallen prey.

Below: A pretty fawn, completely motionless, can blend perfectly with the forest undergrowth, thanks to the spotted markings that they all have.

Above: The chinchilla originated in South America. His thick, soft fur is beautiful to look at and to feel. Unfortunately, this very fur makes him the victim of hunters.

Right: A gray Arctic wolf.

from mountain sickness, or vertigo (dizziness), and he's a fine jumper. The minute he scents danger, he hides in some cranny or mountain crag. He's very big; let's say he's a large, wild, shy sort of sheep. He does have a reputation for aggressiveness, spread around by no less a person than Marco Polo. This famous traveler said that the takin was a fierce beast who was always ready to attack the unwary person. He attacks all right, but his object is not a human being. It's a plant, the bamboo, which is his favorite food.

Perhaps you've noticed that I've already mentioned the scent of danger. That is because the four-legged Alpine creatures, like other animals, have a fine sense of smell. With it they are able to detect danger.

You know that the higher one goes the lower the temperature gets. In the Alps, the temperature falls about 1 degree every 450 feet. In the Caucasus, the temperature falls 1 degree every 500 feet; and in the Andes, 1 degree every 550 feet. Ever-present glaciers and short warm periods virtually limit the Alpine zones to two seasons: summer and winter. The winter is very long, and the summer definitely short. On the Italian Alps, for example, at an altitude of over 10,000 feet, average temperatures of above zero are registered during only 2 months of the year. The mountains are often wrapped in fog and clouds; this is a sign of the great humidity in the region.

HOT AND COLD

The temperature drops as the altitude rises. This divides the vegetation and therefore the animal life into zones. This is clearly shown by the varying kinds of land squirrels we meet as we climb up the American Sierra Nevada mountains.

75

The giant panda, or bamboo, bear has a short muzzle, fur on the soles of his feet, and a thick rough fur divided into black and white areas. Below: Barbary sheep, who live in the mountains of the Sahara, are clever at eluding hunters.

Every region has its Chip and Dales! That's only a manner of speaking, for it is not applicable to all mammals. The attractive panda, you see, is only to be found—well hidden—in the bamboo forests of Tibet, above an altitude of 5,500 feet.

All right, boys and girls, you don't need to make faces at me. I'm not going off into some long scientific discussion. I know you want to hear more about the panda.

THE BLACK AND WHITE TEDDY BEAR

Black and white cat's feet! Now don't worry, I'm still talking about the panda. "Black and white cat's feet" is the translation of the Greek name for the giant panda. It is also called the bamboo bear, and Father David's bear. This animal, shy by nature, lives as I have said before, in the bamboo forests on the high mountains of eastern Tibet and southern China. It has always been extremely rare and little known. Discovered in 1869 by the French naturalist and missionary Arnaud

David (so that's why he's called Father David's bear!), the panda was only recently imported to Europe and America. The only living specimens in captivity are so few you can count them on your fingers.

We think of this attractive animal as a kind of black and white teddy bear. At least, I do. But it really is only a distant relative of the bear, and belongs in fact to the raccoon family. Whether because he is so rare, or because he is so attractive, the panda has been chosen as the symbol of the largest existing organization for wildlife conservation—the World Wildlife Fund. By the way, tell your friends about the need to protect and help our wildlife. Thanks.

As I told you, the panda was discovered a little over a century ago. But it was not until 30 years ago that the panda was introduced into Europe.

In 1939 a hunter took four live pandas out of their natural surroundings and shipped them to London. There's quite a story connected with that. You see, pandas eat chiefly bamboo shoots. Yes, I said shoots. Well, the London zoo, being fresh out of bamboo shoots at the time, ordered

all of its most highly qualified specialists in charge of pandas to come up with—yes, a satisfactory menu. After a few sleepless nights of studying their books (perhaps their cookbooks?) they finally thought of boiling carrots and serving them to the panda on plates of bamboo leaves. The pandas were fooled, ate happily, and the problem was solved.

The lesser, or true, panda is also very fond of bamboo shoots. This animal is sometimes called the cat bear, because he looks like a small bear and acts like a big cat!

LIVING WAY UP

The rough land, the steep mountain slopes, the canyons dug out by the dizzy, rapid mountain torrents and waterfalls, all favor those animals who are mountain climbers. The mountains are the realm of the ibex and wild mountain goat, the mouflon and the chamois. There are rodents, too, such as the marmot in the Alps and the chinchilla in the Andes, who are inhabitants of the mountains.

Because only a few animals are able to survive at high altitudes, there is a great similarity among those living in mountain ranges found in different parts of the earth. The animals living on the highest peaks of the islands of Java or the Philippines are similar to those found on the mountains of central Asia or North Africa. Let's look at someone climbing to meet us. He is a maned sheep, an animal found in North Africa. The male has curved antlers, and no mane (in spite of his name!) but a thick beard almost reaching the ground. All of these sheep are excellent jumpers and climbers. Once they lived in large herds, and specialists believe they are a link between goats and sheep. Today, because of too many greedy hunters, the maned sheep is rare. The Egyptian subspecies is already extinct—this means it has died out—and the same fate awaits the others unless indiscriminate hunting is stopped. Fortunately, maned sheep do live safely in North Africa, and now have been introduced in other parts of the world, such as Canada and the United States where they are well protected by rules and regulations.

THE GREAT JUMPERS

The animals of the mountains are jumpers in every sense of the word. They skip, too, and not only along a mountain path, but skip meals as well. Sorry for the pun, but it's amazing that they can survive on so little food. The Himalayan yak, for example, is content with pasture land so sparse that domestic cattle would die of malnutrition if they had to live on it. Bad weather often forces many mountain animals to migrate periodically into the valleys. The ibex, which in summer lives on the high peaks of the Gran Paradiso in Italy, must descend below the tree line in the winter to find his food. As I told you at the beginning of this chapter, I have one here within reach, and I'll tell you about him before he leaves me.

The mountain goat (above) lives in the mountains of North America. His thick, white fur makes him look quite dumpy and round. The alpine groundhog lives at an altitude of 4500 feet. He is very cautious and able to hear sounds at a great distance and this enables him to escape danger. Right: Snow leopard or irbis. Only a few hundred remain, living in the Himalayan mountains and other parts of Asia at an altitude between 6000 feet and 9000 feet. Its hairy tail of about 3 feet in length is almost as long as the rest of its body.

Master of the rocks and the ravines, the extraordinary ibex has no equal when it comes to agility. He is able to jump across a distance of 24 to 30 feet with the greatest of ease, and over a void—that is, with nothing under him but an empty abyss! Imagine, this male jumper weighs around 220 pounds! That, of course, is the weight of the adult male ibex (the young are like little puffs of cream-colored fur, weighing only about 5 pounds). His horns, about 3 feet in length, weigh about 33 pounds.

Some years ago, this unusual animal almost became extinct. Happily for them —and for us—a few wise men decided to protect these animals. They created a natural habitat where hunting was and still is forbidden. Wasn't that a wonderful thing to do!

Sorry, boys and girls, sometimes I can't help showing the sentimental side of my nature. I do love animals. Believe it or not, this is not only because I happen to be one of them. I believe firmly that all that lives should be respected: both to maintain the balance of nature and also for the good of man himself. At this moment I'm thinking of Albert Schweitzer. This man, who won the Nobel peace prize, can express it better than I can. At the end of each tiring day spent with the sick, Dr. Schweitzer closed his prayers with these words: Protect and bless all living things; defend them from evil and let them sleep in peace.

IN SNOW AND ICE

Polar regions, here I come. Yes, friends, it's still me, Donald Duck. You'll have to take my word for it, because you can't see me. I'm shut up in an igloo.

No, that won't do, the editors tell me. I can't open up a chapter by being shut up. So out I come, through the window. It's on the ground floor, so I didn't hurt myself.

But I've already explored a bit up here near the North Pole, about four slides and seven headlong falls, by my count. But I've really prepared a great program for us, so let's make a start. As usual, we will first take a good look at our surroundings.

In many ways, living conditions near the poles are like those in the high mountains. The average daily and yearly temperatures fall the higher you climb and the closer you get to the poles. Here, the drop in temperatures means that precipitation is almost always in the form of snow. The accumulation of snow helps bring about the formation of glaciers. Short summers are followed by long winters, just as in the mountain regions.

Around the poles, even the areas that are at sea level remain almost constantly covered by snow and ice. But when the sun shines through and when the snow is blown away by the wind, the ground warms up. Then the top coat of ice that covers the ground melts, at least for a short time.

POLES APART

The Arctic polar regions are those surrounding the North Pole. The Antarctic regions are those around the South Pole. It is there that the dear old penguins live. This should help you to remember which is which! Penguins equal South Pole. No penguins equal North Pole. All right, let's go on. If you will follow me for a bit, you'll learn some more, my friends. But let me point out to you the really big difference between the two polar regions. Antarctica is a great landmass. In fact we talk of the South Pole as the Antarctic continent. The Arctic, on the other hand, is a huge mass of frozen water.

In Antarctica, the winters are not as cold as in the Arctic, although the summers are much colder. Because summer temperatures always remain below that necessary for the growth of vegetation, in Antarctica we find only two flowering plants and a few kinds of moss and algae. Vertebrates (animals with backbones) do not live in the interior of Antarctica. Birds, particularly the penguins, are found mostly on the coasts. Some kinds of mammals live there too.

Even the invertebrates (animals without backbones) are scarce in this part of the world. Few animals can be found at any distance from the penguin colonies. But, after some searching, it is possible to

come across a few primitive insects such as wingless flies and some single-celled animals. These tiny inhabitants of Antarctica live actively for a few days of the year only, and then spend the rest of their lives half-frozen, in a state of semi-sleep. The only mammals that come regularly to the coast of Antarctica to reproduce are certain species of seal. But at this point, stop! With the editors' permission, I believe I'll have a swim. Anyone join me for a lesson? Come on, I'm going to a very special school—a school run by seals.

SCHOOL FOR SEALS

A newborn seal faces one problem right away. He is an animal whose only hope of survival (he eats fish) and defense (his

Above: The sharp pointed snout of a young otter.
Below: A Greenland seal pup, still covered by
the thick white fur which makes him the target
of bloody hunts. He is anxiously waiting for his
mother, whose dark head is emerging from a hole
in the ice. Greenland seals are sea-going and
migratory. They'd rather live on floating icebergs
than on land.

best defense is escape) lies in the sea. So guess what he must do?

The answer is, you say, that he must learn to swim. How obvious: well, yes, but try telling that to the baby seals. The water is cold when they are told to go in and they all set up a tremendous squeal. Mother seal knows that one is born able to swim. Since for seals it is a matter of necessity, she tries first of all to encourage her young to follow her into the water.

If they don't, well, she knocks them in with her flipper. Then she dives quickly after them and swims back and forth around them, ready to come to their help if needed.

THE SEAL AND HIS COUSINS

The word "seal" is a general heading for three groups of water animals: the true seal and sea elephant; the otter and sea lion; and the walrus. Along with excellent swimming ability, all of these mammals can sometimes move with great agility on the land. Males of all the species have a warlike temperament. They must protect a large number of wives and children and so they take for themselves part of the coastline. No rival is permitted to approach this area and the male seal tries to keep them off with fierce yells. If, however, another male approaches unafraid, the defender male will fight until the last drop of blood has been shed. All members of the seal family have a strong feeling for the family and they live in herds, especially during mating season.

Other mammals found only in the Arctic are the musk ox and the polar bear. The polar bear, or white bear, lives for most of the year on the Arctic Ocean ice pack. His daily menu features certain local specialities such as various kinds of seal. But during the summer the polar bear must, because of the breaking of the ice, find shelter on land where he is forced to be content with whatever he can find by way of food. Usually this consists of roots and berries.

The domain of the polar bear is limited to areas where he can have solid ground under foot as much as possible. Usually, the bear cubs are born in March or April after the female has retreated into a den.

It does seem strange that this animal, which lives so far from human settlements,

A colony of sea lions photographed on the coast of the Pribilof Islands in the Bering Sea. The fur of these animals is valuable. In May, at the beginning of the mating season, the males reach the island. They are joined by their females in mid-June. Top, right: Three sea lions sunning themeslves on a beach. Center: A mother with a pup. The pups are born between August and December and are cared for by the mother. Bottom: A sturdy specimen. The male differs from the female in his enormous size and thickness of mustache.

is on the verge of dying out. It was a long time ago, around the year 1600, when the decline began. This was when ships began to sail back and forth in Arctic waters. As whale hunting became less profitable, merchant fleets devoted their time to capturing seals. This led in turn to the hunting of polar bears.

Up to that time only the Eskimo had killed the bear, and then only when it was a matter of survival. Their hunting had little impact on the population of this animal. For centuries the desolate polar regions had provided safe refuge for the white bear (polar bear, remember?). But with the introduction of firearms, and an increase in modern means of transportation, including the airplane, the survival of this unique species of mammal is seriously threatened. The fact that he lives outside any territorial waters, in what one might call a rather damp "no man's land," makes control over hunting and trapping enormously difficult if not outright impossible.

These two pages show the polar bear, one of the largest carnivorous animals in the world.

A herd of walrus, with their characteristic long tusks, basking in the coastal sun.

In 1965, at Fairbanks, Alaska, the first national conference on polar bears was held. Its purpose was to study a plan that would offer the interested nations (the United States, the Soviet Union, Canada, Norway, and Denmark) a means of guaranteeing the polar bear's survival. Agreement was reached. This encouraged scientific research on the life cycle of the polar bear, research necessary for bringing about a plan that would permit hunting while preventing the extinction of the animal.

The same international guarantee protects the survival of another Arctic mammal: the walrus. This distinct relative of the seal can grow as long as 12 feet and weigh as much as 2,600 pounds. The females are smaller than the males, whose tusks are sometimes as long as 3¼ feet. The walrus uses his front tusks for digging and finding mollusks—his chief food —as well as for fighting and defending himself.

Walrus usually live in large mixed herds of a thousand or more, and on small islands along the rocky coasts or on floating icebergs.

A Canadian law of 1931 restricted the hunting of walrus to Eskimos and the few whites living in the region. This law also forbade export of the animal's skin and ivory tusks in their natural states. Further restrictions governing hunting were enacted in 1949. Under these rules only a few head could be killed each year. Walrus are also well protected under Danish and Norwegian law. In the Soviet Union, walrus hunting is limited mainly to Eskimos. Today the walrus has a better life. This shows that good will and the joint efforts of different peoples can encourage the enjoyment and use of natural resources without destroying them.

A CLEVER DEFENDER

Coming toward us with a measured pace and looking almost totally indifferent to everything around him is the musk ox. He has the appearance of knowing a thing

The fur of polar animals not only changes color with seasonal weather changes but may sometimes— as in the case of the arctic fox pup puff up to keep him warm in the snow, thanks to a thick, insulating layer of air.

or two, and above all, of being extremely sure of himself. The musk ox, or musky, of all the herbivores (plant-eating animals) in the Arctic, ranges the farthest north. He is really a living legend, a survivor of the Ice Age. And we see him today just as he appeared to the painters of the prehistoric Stone Age. The musk ox species has been able to survive long centuries of polar climate thanks to the protection of his extremely thick fur. And he has always managed to resist the attacks by wolves because of very fine defense strategy. As soon as their enemy is sighted or scented, the musk oxen join ranks and form a square. In the center of the square are the females and offspring. The males form the outer ranks, their horns pointed out ready to strike.

If the wolves have any sense at all, they'll act as though they see nothing and go on about their business. If they insist— well, they're going to lose their skins. But, sad to say, the poor musk ox often loses his own skin when he is confronted by man and his guns.

THE ESKIMO'S BEST FRIEND

Hey, my friends. Take a look down there. Isn't that a pack of dogs racing toward us at full speed? Hey, you there! No, boys and girls, I don't mean you. I'm talking to the dogs here.

What dears they are and so obedient! When ordered to they wouldn't move an inch. Ah, there, show me your identification: Siberian husky. Height: 2 feet. Color of fur: light or dark brown. Profession? Sleigh pullers. Residence? North Pole. Distinguishing features: one dried fish daily on the average, between the teeth, and two bright blue eyes.

Well, my friends and readers, I've just introduced you to the fantastic husky. This is the marvelous Eskimo dog, so generous and faithful that he will risk his life for his master. He is the famous four-legged friend of the men who live near the Pole. He works for them and almost never tires.

It is no coincidence that the huskies are sticking their muzzles into this chapter on bears. Why? Because they know that the Eskimo fur traders could never survive without them in these polar regions. Eskimo dog, or sleigh dog, are vague terms, and we can do better than that. Actually, there are four main kinds of dogs who pull sleighs: the Samoyede, the Alaskan Malamute, the Greenlander, and the Siberian husky. The Siberian husky is the smallest and fastest of all the sleigh dogs. The Samoyede, with its double coat of white, cream, or light tan-colored fur, has been purebred for a very long time. Originally the Samoyeds were the constant companions of the hardy nomads who roamed the Siberian tundra. Then these noble dogs were used for herding reindeer, hunting bear, and pulling sleighs. They were so highly regarded that they slept in their owners' tents as members of the family. Just take a look at those dogs in the picture. Aren't they magnificent! You can almost hear them bark.

THEY LIVE IN WATER BUT NEED AIR

Well, as I was saying, unexpectedly, in this chapter I was handed the enormous job of telling you all about sea mammals. There is hardly space enough here to tell you about this vast matter. As soon as I get started, I get my line all tangled. I'll cut it, and this unnecessary chatter as well, and begin.

The only mammals that are completely adapted to underwater living—in fact they are not able to exist outside of water—are the cetaceans. That is, the whales and dolphins. They are mammals whose bodies have undergone outstanding evolutionary changes: their front legs have become fins and their rear legs have completely disappeared. The tail has become a flat, horizontal fin used to propel them through the water. They also have a rear fin, called the dorsal fin, of fatty tissue which, while it has nothing to do with a fish dorsal, does serve to show the similarity between fish and cetacean.

This resemblance deceived man for centuries. Whales and dolphins were considered fish, even though it was known that many of them were furry! It was even more of an error since they did know that whales and dolphins suckled their young. It wasn't until the 17th century that the great English naturalist John Ray

classified these "animals" as mammals. There is no doubt that these species originated from land forms. This development can be seen when the species is in the embryo stage. At this time, their jaws begin to grow, as in all mammals. As the embryo develops the front paws become pectoral fins and the rear ones disappear. The nostrils, appearing earlier on the front of the snout, as in all mammals, gradually move towards the top of the head and become the famous "air holes."

A WHALE OF AN ANIMAL

Like other mammals cetaceans must breathe air. They do this because they have lungs, not gills. You've probably read about the water spout of the whale and sperm whale. Or maybe you've seen it on the movie screen. Well, it is really nothing more than water vapor under pressure, which is exhaled from the lungs and expelled through the air holes when the animals surface to breathe. Their ability to remain under water without breathing for long periods of time is well known. This is possible, at least partly, because of their enormous lung capacity. A big whale can store more than 2,114 quarts of air

93

and, because of his great oxygen reserve, is able to dive as deep as 1,100 feet.

Let me tell you a few more interesting facts about our whales. For example, they seem to be closely related to cows and other ruminants, or cud chewers. Whales have several stomachs, as do cattle. We have also found out that they have the same sleep patterns as cattle. Whales nap briefly during the day and night. Between those naps they are active.

No one knows how or why the whale's land-living ancestors first took to water. Perhaps it was to escape from their fierce enemies. More likely it was to find food. Anyway, over a period of millions of years these animals gradually changed. They developed in ways that fitted them better to life in the water.

Early in this development they may have acted like stout-tailed otters or beavers. Later they may have behaved like seals, coming ashore mainly to produce their young. Finally, they must have given up entirely this dependence on land, bearing and nursing their young without ever coming ashore. But, even now, whales must rise to the surface in order to breathe. And unlike fishes, whales keep a constant body temperature very close to that of man and many other land mammals.

Water is a medium that carries heat away from a body much faster than air does. A human being, for example, becomes chilled in water at a temperature that would be quite comfortable in air. A larger animal, such as a whale, has a smaller surface area in relation to its total bulk. In other words it has less body surface from which heat may be lost. So a whale's giant size helps it to save its body heat.

Whales have another adaptation that saves body heat. Each whale has under its skin a thick layer of fatty tissue, called

blubber. This coat of fat helps the whale stay warm.

Man has hunted whales for commercial profit since ancient times. But it was not until the 16th-century voyages of European explorers that whales were in danger. While on their way the voyagers came across large schools of cetaceans, and from that time, whaling fleets were formed to hunt them. These fleets became more and more efficient and destructive, pitilessly slaughtering these peaceful, extraordinary lords of the seas. So thorough was this wholesale killing that today some species,

Left: The killer whale lives in chilly waters. He is a savage killer and does not hesitate to attack a whale of much larger size. His head is very small compared to the rest of his body. His mouth has from 40 to 56 teeth. Above: Dolphins always put on a good act. Here, they show how high they can jump for a snack.

such as the blue whale, are nearly extinct. The existence of all whales is seriously threatened. In spite of the efforts of the International Whaling Commission, founded in 1946, which has set restrictions on hunting whales, it is not possible to tell whether these gigantic sea mammals will survive for future generations.

A BIG FAMILY

The cetaceans are divided into two groups. The first, the Mysticeti, includes whales and rorquals (12 species in all, including the red whale and fin back). Whales and rorquals have no teeth but a peculiar set of blades called whalebones. These hang from the roof of the mouth and filter out the small shellfish, which are the main food for these cetaceans.

Among the largest of the species, and almost extinct, is the blue rorqual. It is 60 feet in length and weighs some 50 tons —a little bit like 25 elephants put together!

In fact, it is the largest animal that has ever existed on the earth. The dinosaur was by comparison a lightweight of a few tons only.

The second group of cetaceans are the Odontocetans. These mammals are equipped with teeth, and feed on fish and rather large prey. The group includes species often differing from one another: the sperm whale, the zifi, the dolphins, the globicephales, the beluga, the narwhal, the killer whale, the Amazon River Inia, the Ganges dolphin, and last, the very rare Chinese lake dolphin. As far as I can tell, he is found only in Tungting Lake in Hunan province.

One of the most curious of all cetaceans is the narwhal, found in the Arctic seas. Full-grown narwhals have but two teeth horizontally placed in the jaw. In the male the left-hand one grows to become a serrated tusk sometimes 9 feet in length. No one knows what this tusk is for, and the fact that only the male has it refutes the theory that the tusks serve to spear prey or to break the ice.

The killer whale, the most terrifying monster of the seas, actually is a member

Above: The elegant pirouette of a humpback whale, or Megaptera. These members of the cetaceans live in large schools. Next to the humpback is the black Globicephalus, or pilot whale. Below: The narwhal is a cetacean that has a long tooth, shaped like a harpoon.

of the dolphin family. These huge beings are to be found all over the world. Males are often 27 feet long. The killer whale has an impressive set of teeth, which allow him to feed not only on fish but on birds and sea mammals as well. He savagely attacks seals, otters, and rorquals. The killer whale even attacks other whales without the slightest hesitation.

But in spite of their unusual savagery, killer whales are rather docile when in captivity, and even make friends with

man. One killer whale in Seattle's aquarium not only allowed visitors to ride on his back, but even seemed to enjoy giving them a ride.

When it comes to the question of intelligence, however, it is the dolphin who is by far the most interesting of the cetaceans. The brain of the dolphin, believe it or not, has more convolutions than man's. Intelligence seems to be related to the surface foldings, or convolutions, of the brain. It is amazing how many tricks the dolphin is able to learn with no trouble at all. Many of the incredible tales of the dolphin's ability must be true. It has been proved that at times dolphins do help their own sick or wounded companions by lifting them out of the water so that their nostrils reach the surface and permit them to breathe.

Very recently studies have confirmed the ability of the dolphin to imitate human speech, even though their version is so fast that we are only able to distinguish the words by means of special instruments.

Before I forget, I'd like to point out one more interesting piece of information.

Dolphins and other large cetaceans, such as sharks, are often escorted by schools of pilot fish. These are small fish that often follow larger fish around (and sometimes even ships) in the hopes of picking up a meal from their leftovers. And many times these clever little pilot fish do find more than enough to eat.

I told you, boys and girls, that our visit to the whales and dolphins would be worth it. And now the night is about to cover everything with its dark blue velvet cape studded with stars. But we can't sleep yet. There is a new voyage ahead of us—a truly fascinating one. We shall now see the mammals of the air.

A school of dolphins. These cetaceans (who have 260 teeth!) show unusual ability for communicating among themselves and also have a high level of intelligence. Other qualities of the dolphin are sturdiness, agility, sociability, and affection for offspring.

THEY WHO SEE BEST IN THE DARK

What can I say, my friends? How can I begin, when I know perfectly well that as soon as you turn the page you'll jump out of your skins? I took a look myself and believe me, I hit the ceiling. I feel sure, however, that once you've read a paragraph or two, you'll be fascinated by these interesting little mammals. Since they are particularly useful to agriculture and to the balance of nature, they are protected by law. Let me proceed at once with the introductions.

Here are the bats. They are the only mammals that can fly. Now you are thinking of man with his airplanes? So let me say it another way: the bats are the only mammals that move through the air with wings. They can do this because their bodies have gone through some structural changes. The front legs, with highly developed "fingers," except for the thumb, support the wing membrane. This membrane is made of a thin, elastic skin, which is webbed and connects front legs, rear legs, and a tail. The rear fingers are free, allowing the bats to cling to branches and other objects in their characteristic upside down position.

The chest muscles of this flying mammal are particularly well developed, so that the bat can move its wings in a somewhat different fashion than the bird. The wing moves up and down, and round about as well, in a circular fashion. The frequency of movement varies according to wing size.

The common, or garden, night bat is able to fly as fast as 30 miles an hour. The so-called rat-eared bat, with his wider and more rounded wings, is not able to fly faster than 10 miles an hour. Some of the smaller kinds of bats are more agile than birds, with the possible exception of the hummingbird. Like the hummingbird, these bats eat flowers and are able to glide or remain still in the air over the same spot. The larger type of bat, on the other hand, takes advantage of ascending air currents. He flies with outspread wings, with the same ease as the sea gull or a hovering predatory bird. Wings closed, bats are able to climb and run on land, just like other four-footed animals and with far greater ease than we might expect. Isn't this all getting more interesting by the minute?

101

FLYING BY EAR

Among the fossils that have been dug up are the perfectly formed specimens of bats that date back over 50,000,000 years. Here is proof of the evolutionary success of the bat, a mammal, which has shared the kingdom of the air with birds from almost the dawn of time. Thanks to their ease of movement, they are to be found in many parts of the world. There are no bats at the poles and in the deserts. In these regions they are unable to find the flying insects on which they live.

In the dark world inhabited by nearly all kinds of bats, sight is certainly not very important. On the other hand, it is clear that in order to capture the very swift insects on which they feed, the bats must have a capacity for, and sureness in flying that is exceptional. It was the great Italian zoologist, Lazzaro Spallanzani, who first discovered in the 1780's which of their senses bats used for night flying. In an experiment, he strung threads all around a room and let the bats fly freely. The bats flew through the maze without touching the threads. He noted also that even with their eyelids sealed they had no trouble. Greatly surprised and excited, Spallanzani continued his experiments and found that when their ears were plugged with wax, the bats bumped into one another and got entangled in the threads. The scientist concluded that the sense of hearing is more important to a bat in flight than his sense of touch or sight. Sad to say, few people took Spallanzani seriously, and his experiments were largely ignored for centuries. This sort of thing has happened before in history and unfortunately continues to happen.

ANIMAL RADAR

It was not until very many years later that a Dutchman and an American, working independently and using the most modern techniques, were able to prove that bats emit high frequency sounds. These sounds are not heard by the human ear. But as they bounce off various objects the sounds are heard by bats. This "bouncing" of sound waves is the basic principle of radar. The scientists merely applied to radio equipment the system which nature had been using for millions of years. The sound waves, also known as "ultra sounds," or high frequency vibrations, are emitted through the mouths of the bats. When the sounds hit an obstacle, they bounce back and are picked up by the sensitive ears of the bats. The bat judges the distance between himself and the object by the time it takes for the sound to bounce back.

Many bats, such as the "horseshoe bat" or the "vampire" bat, have straight membranes on their noses. For many years scientists were unaware of the function of these membranes. Then the scientists discovered a connection between the larynx and the nasal cavity. They realized that the membranes acted as frequency modulators for ultrasonic noise vibrations, which the bats are able to emit even with their mouths closed. Furthermore, because bats hunt their prey in the dark, they often catch small objects or insects

Right: A bat at rest, with hanging feet and folded wings. A talented flyer, he can go as far as 62 miles from home, batting his wings 16–20 times a second.

which are poisonous. To avoid this, they put into use a sort of second nose.

HOW BATS LIVE

There are nearly a thousand different species or kinds of bats. They are spread all over the world, but you're not going to find them in the desert and polar regions. I've already told you that, didn't I? But I thought it important enough so I'm telling you that fact again. Each kind of bat has habits that are different from other species. Yet with all of their differences the various species have many things in common.

Bats are usually social animals; that is, they live in groups. But bats are not like other social animals, such as bees and prairie dogs. Bees and prairie dogs always make their own dwellings. But bats look for a cave or a hollow tree in which to make their home.

If you see one bat flying into a cave, you can be fairly sure that there are other bats inside. In some caves thousands of bats crowd together on walls and ceilings. In such large colonies scientists often find bats of one kind sharing a cave with a few bats of different species. Smaller colonies numbering only 10 or 12 bats may live in a hollow tree. But, getting back to caves for a moment, do you know about the Carlsbad Caverns in New Mexico? Well, they are one of the most famous groups of caves in the world. Now listen to this, the Carlsbad Caverns are the home to at least 9,000,000 Tadarida bats. How about that!

Caves and hollow trees are not the only places where bats live. Some bats simply roost in trees, hanging like leaves from twigs and branches. Two kinds of tropical bats make little tents from palm leaves. Such a bat slits the leaf with his teeth and then hangs inside the folds.

And now, struck dumb at all that I've revealed and astonished at how much I've managed to learn about these strange mammals, I shall retreat. I am so overcome with emotion, I'll have to leave you. Besides, I want to be the first to move into the next chapter.

Opposite page: This Asian bat clearly doesn't find this upside down rest position at all tiring. Firmly clutching a branch with his rear claws, he not only sleeps, but can also hibernate for months in the same place. Above: Most bats eat insects. Others eat both fruit and insects. This long-nosed bat, shown here, is sipping flower nectar.

THE ANIMALS WHO LIVE WITH US

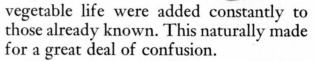

Perhaps I should have mentioned them before, right at the beginning, when I introduced myself and told you I was to be your guide on this long, fascinating adventure-filled journey through the mammal world. I did think of it, really, but decided to keep this as an ace up my sleeve. But now, dear friends, the time has come to lay my cards on the table. This chapter is dedicated to the animals the whole world loves, those creatures who live close to you and for you.

But be patient with me for just another minute or two. I want to tell you a little about the famous Swedish naturalist Karl von Linne—or Carolus Linnaeus (the Latin form of his name) as he is generally called. We have mentioned his name before.

Linnaeus (1707–78) invented a system for subdividing and classifying plants and animals. Almost from the time man began to notice the plant and animal life around him, no one except that early Greek philosopher, Aristotle, thought of cataloguing this life according to the characteristics they had in common.

This problem of classification became even greater after the voyages to the newly discovered regions of the world. Travelers, merchants, and explorers continued to bring back word of plants and animals never seen before. Sometimes they even brought back the very plants and animals. So in this way thousands and thousands of new forms of animal and vegetable life were added constantly to those already known. This naturally made for a great deal of confusion.

What was it that Linnaeus did? He thought up a very simple system. In 1735, Linnaeus published a book called *Systema Naturae* ("The System of Nature"). This book explained his system. Each plant and animal was to have two Latin names, one telling its group (genus) and the other its kind (species). This made it simple for scientists to recognize the name of a plant or animal, no matter what its common name. The system of classification was quickly accepted throughout Europe.

This Linnaeus was quite a fellow. The true scientist, if there ever was one! Whenever he saw a collection of things, he had a burning desire to arrange them in an orderly way. He became famous for his systems of arranging animals, minerals, and most of all, plants. The *Systema Naturae* was only the beginning of his work in classifying living things. When Linnaeus died in 1778, he was a man greatly honored and respected. He had become known as the "prince of botanists." A botanist is a man who studies plants. By the way, Linnaeus wrote in Latin because in his day most scientific books were written in that language.

Well, that little side step took longer than I thought. But I think it was necessary to make things clear, don't you? And it also gave me the chance to salute that great Swedish naturalist.

FROM HUNTER TO HERDSMEN

Now, boys and girls, this is a good time to say "let's start from the beginning." That is, let's jump backwards in time and see what went on thousands upon thousands of years ago.

Primitive man was a gatherer and a hunter. He picked berries and fruit. Many tribes were nomadic, moving from place to place in search of the animals they hunted or fleeing from bad weather. When man made tools out of stone, he also took the very first important steps on the road to progress. These tools were

*Above, left: Belgian sheepdog, Tervueren variety.
The use of these and all other shepherd dogs dates
back to prehistoric times. The Belgium shepherd
belongs to the so-called wolf dog group.
Left, below: A pointer. These dogs have a highly
developed sense of smell and are used for hunting.
Above, right: Setter—a typical hunting dog
famous for his beauty and hunting skill, bred by
the English as early as the 16th century. Below him
is a brindled boxer, a close relative of the bulldog,
and one of the most recently pedigreed (1895).
He is considered a great friend of children. Below
him is the Great Dane.*

weapons and utensils, and they were crudely shaped. But they were the best that man could make at that time. What was our caveman able to do with these tools? He was trying to make a better life for himself. Hasn't man always done that down through the ages? And since the caveman knew that plants and animals were necessary for his survival, man turned his attention to them.

THE FAITHFUL FRIEND

It is not possible to know for sure whether man first grew plants or tamed animals, because the development of a simple kind of agriculture could have taken place without the use of animals. But it is almost certain that the first friend of man was the dog, or rather, the forefather of most dogs known today: the jackal. In ancient times, great packs of jackals gathered around the hunters' fires, waiting to eat the leftovers.

Konrad Lorentz, a well-known authority on animal behavior, tells us: "One of the most intelligent deeds of those prehistoric hunters was the tossing of a piece of meat to some fearless jackal roaming around, not far from the fire. This was the beginning of the friendship between dog and man." The jackal is really nothing more than a wild dog, somewhat more timid than the wolf. For this very reason, it is easier to tame him. Early man found it quite comforting to have the jackal following him around. Let me explain why. When the hunting tribes moved across open land, nightfall must have made the outdoors more threatening and frightening than it was during the day. The excited barking of the jackals warned against any approaching danger, whether it was an animal or an enemy tribe.

At first, the relationship between man and this "near-dog" jackal must have been one where both helped each other in the ways I have just mentioned. But when some pack leader, made more courageous by knowing that man was not a danger to him, was able to lead a hunter to some wounded animal hiding in the underbrush, a new relationship was established. Of course, it might not have taken place just exactly as I have told you. But the fact remains that the first dogs were used by man for hunting. Our studies tell us that the first dogs were not used for defense until much later.

We can date the taming of dogs back 10,000 years. Ancient sculptures show us that the Assyrians had huge mastifflike dogs in 600 B.C. We are sure that the Egyptians had dogs. The Afghan hound of today probably originated in Sinai, because it is mentioned more than once in Egyptian records dated 4,000 B.C. They are also pictured on a vase of that period. Legend has it that this was the breed of

Opposite page, above: Two giant schnauzers. These dogs are of German origin and love to travel. During the days of the horse and carriage, they ran between the horses legs, practically under their hooves. Opposite page, below: A Dalmation, an excellent watchdog and highly prized for his black and white coat. He was once called a "carriage dog," and now sometimes a firehouse dog. Above, left: A chow chow, supposedly introduced into Europe from China in 1879. Next to him is a group of lively, intelligent cocker spaniels. The parade is closed by a basketful of white Persian kittens.

dog saved by Noah. Good old Noah, just before the Flood, took a couple of these hounds into the Ark. Another legend tells us that a leak sprung in the Ark and that these dogs stopped it up with their noses. This explains why their noses are always so cold and damp! Oh, just a moment. Malachi the Cat wants a word with us. What's that? Ah, yes, absolutely! Right, I'll tell them immediately. . . . Of all our animal friends, the one which knows best how to show his love for man is the dog. And if Malachi says it . . . then we'd better believe it.

HOLY CATS

Not everyone will agree that the cat is really a domestic animal. Certain kinds of cats were known and worshiped in ancient Egypt around 1600 B.C. There seems little question that they descended from the wild European cat, which even today is not easily tamed.

Well, boys and girls, don't believe that a mere flick of the tail disposes of all of Malachi's ancestors. I should say not. That little cat is too much a part of my daily life. If I didn't say more about that extraordinary, regal, and arrogant race to which he and 50,000,000 other cats belong, I believe he'd be offended. In Ancient Egypt, the cat was worshiped and protected by special laws. Anyone who dared offend their feline majesties was punished by death. Ulp! But to tell you the honest truth, this came about because the Egyptians, after taming the cat, had trained it to guard the warehouses of wheat against rats. They did such a good job that the Egyptians considered them sacred and worthy of worship.

It must have been about that time that our cats took on their strange, aloof, and sort of proud look. This was after they found out that Confucius, the great Chinese philosopher, had a favorite cat. In

Opposite page, above: The tabby cat (Syrian or tiger cat) is the most common. While they are usually of gray and yellow stripes, they may also be beige, brown, dark gray, silver and blue in color. Opposite page, below: Siamese cats, with tan fur, black mask, paws and tail, are very aggressive in spite of their sweet and bright blue eyes. Right: Przhewalski horse, plentiful on the steppes of Siberia and China. It is one of the untamed species of horse still left. Below: The graceful canter of a horse running free. Today even the so-called wild horses (like the famous mustangs, and the cimarrones of South America) are actually the descendents of domesticated horses returned to their wild state.

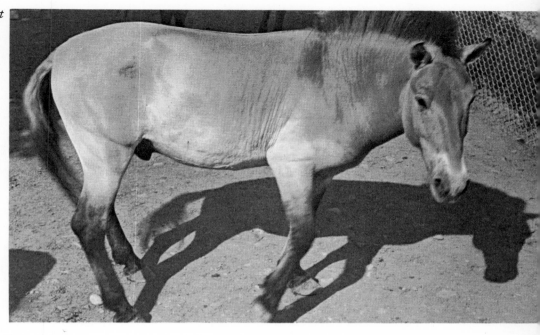

113

Japan during the same period cats were trained to guard the temples and to defend the precious manuscripts kept there from enemy paws. I mean hands.

Cats were always kept on a leash in Japan, until 1600 A.D. when an imperial decree allowed them to run free. This was done in order to help the people catch the small rats that were ruining the silk industry.

Perhaps this explains why even today the Japanese hold cats in such high regard. It seems—but don't let Malachi hear us—that the Japanese cat is the most loved in the world. Meow!

Left: A group of donkeys grazing—on the island of Asinara near Sardinia, in the Mediterranean. According to estimates, Italy and Spain are superior in the breeding of donkeys. This "friend of man" is highly important in regions which are arid and rough in terrain, and where agriculture is poor. Above: Horses of the fjords, resting. Famous throughout Norway for their strength, these horses are used for transportation in mountainous regions. Their hide is thicker than most, and this helps them bear the great cold. These horses of the fjords belong to a race of cart horses, so called because their bone structure is heavy, their trunk strong, the legs short and thick.

Opposite page: The Andalusian mule. The mule is the son of a donkey and a female horse. It is a rather rough animal, well able to endure hardship and rough climate.

115

ON THE GRAZING LANDS

Let's leave his Majesty the Cat to his silks and laces, and go for a walk in the pastures to relax. Look, boys and girls, there's a piece of wool caught on a branch. Good! We're certainly on the right path. We must be approaching a very important group of animals. Without these animals man would never have been able to make it up to now.

Sheep, goats, oxen, and pigs, like all other animals before they became part of

Top: The antelope's large dreamy eyes are particularly evident in this picture of a cub.
Lower, left: Splendid example of the Italian ox.
*Above: Australian ram
of the famous Merino breed, with characteristic curved horns.*

the world in which we live, were once wild. Their way of life was a free one. They roamed about seemingly endless pastures. But these wild animals were fated to serve a new purpose for man, as he moved from his early stages as a hunter to a higher development. The time came when man had a family, some rough implements, a roof, and the power of using fire to his advantage. A new day had come for the sheep, goats, pigs, and oxen. No more wild racing through the boundless prairies. The days and nights of the old freedom had come to an end.

Below: Black and white Dutch cattle, called Frisians. This breed was brought to the United States and has developed into the best milk giving cows in the world. In Holland, these cattle are the wealth of the country people and dairy owners, and they receive the best of care. For example, they are protected against cold morning mists by old blankets or jute covers. Their stalls are built according to scientific methods and the animals live in perfect hygienic conditions. Holsteins, as they are called in America, can produce up to 6800 quarts of milk in a year.

It is difficult to establish exactly when goats and sheep were tamed. The skeletons found near ancient settlements do not differ greatly from those of the wild species. Some scholars believe that goats were tamed as far back as 7000 B.C. The earliest goats were animals of the steep hills and mountains of Asia. Later they spread to North Africa and parts of Eastern Europe. Sheep were probably tamed about the same time as goats were. In a fairly short time, particularly in the Near East, the sheep became more numerous than the goats.

Pigs were also tamed very early. We

Left: Sheep breeding in Europe generally is decreasing in the plains. In the mountain regions sheep breeding still represents a source of income, because many Alpine pastures are unfit for use by cattle. Above: Maremma oxen grazing.

do not know exactly when the domestication, or taming, of cattle took place. We are talking now of oxen and cows.

HAVE A SEAT AND RIDE

An animal also very close to our hearts is the horse . . . and here he comes! Where can we find a more noble animal? A more brave and handsome one? Where can we find another animal who has helped man so much in the making of history?

All right, I can imagine what you are

Above: African oxen in a Masai village in Kenya. This animal is a cross between the Mediterranean ox and the zebu, which reached Africa (Egypt) from India about 4000 years ago. African cattle give very little milk (3-4 quarts per day) because of the poor pastureland on which they graze.
Below: Bulls grazing in Andalusia, Spain. These animals, reared in a semi-wild state, are the ones used for bull fighting.

trying to say. You're correct, too. All animals, from the smallest to the biggest, from the handsomest to the ugliest, from the gentlest to the most ferocious, are necessary for making up the marvelous world of nature. It would be logical if we talked about all the animals in the same way. But you have to agree that some animals are closer to our hearts than others.

Not much is known about when or how the donkey and the horse were tamed. Scientists tend to think that the horse was first used as a domestic animal on the Eurasian steppes between the Ukraine and Pakistan between 3000 and 2500 B.C. The ancient Sumerians in Mesopotamia left no record of having

Below: The white llama. The vicuna, the guanaco, and the llama all live in South America, though they belong to the camel family. The llama was domesticated in ancient times. Reared as a beast of burden, he is used also as a source of wool and meat.

Above: A herd of sheep grazing on the island of Texel in the extreme north of Holland. A green cheese famous in the north is made from their milk. Below, left: A herd of camels. Right: A majestic Mehari. The difference between the camel and dromedary is small. Both are able to live in extremely dry climates; both have one or two humps, which they use to store water. Both have a rubbery cushion under their feet, which allows them to walk over sand and rough ground. What's different is the coats of each animal. The dromedary's fur is not as thick or as wooly as the camel's, because he lives in a warm climate.

A picture of a water buck. These animals avoid forests to live on open plains near streams and rivers. They are shy and very fast. Their long legs carry them at dazzling speed.

horses before 1800 B.C. The Egyptians first used this animal in 1675 B.C. On the other hand, the wild donkey was used by the Sumerians to pull their chariots of war. Our modern domestic donkey is the ancestor of the wild African donkey, which was tamed around 3200 B.C. in the Nile Valley, and later put to use in Mesopotamia and Palestine. The Asian wild donkey, however, cannot be considered the forefather of the animal we know today.

Although the camel of Persia, with two humps, was already domesticated 1000 years before Christ, we know almost nothing about the history of the African and Arabian dromedary.

Here I am again, boys and girls. Never have a few moments of separation seemed so long! It was quite a ride, too. Now I'd like to tell you something: the real forefather of our saddle and cart horses was the *equus Przewalski* that is, the horse (*equus* is the Latin word for horse) discovered by the Russian explorer Nikolaj Mickhailovich Przewalski while traveling in Mongolia. This horse was called *kertag* or *kortag* and lived in "the country of animals," the Mongolian name for that part of their country.

It would have been a shame not to have been able to trace back to the forefather of one of man's closest friends. And so once more we must let man pay his due respects to his four-legged friend. Nature, that incredibly marvelous force, is generous to those who love her creatures large and small.

THE END OF THE JOURNEY—FOR NOW

I believe that you, my friends, have enjoyed this very swift gallop through the world of mammals as much as I have. I might even say we've found it an exciting experience.

Together we have met the animals in their own natural surroundings and learned something about them. In order for the meeting between the animals and us to take place, we had to be moved by a feeling of love for all the creatures that live in our world. I know that you have this love in your hearts, because you've been the best traveling companions anyone could ask for.

Your Donald, one who knows he has your love,

With affection,

INDEX

Note: Page numbers in italics refer to pictures.